CBS NewsBreak 6

CBS ニュースブレイク 6

Nobuhiro Kumai　　Stephen Timson

StreamLine

Web 動画・音声ファイルのストリーミング再生について

CD マーク及び Web 動画マークがある箇所は、PC、スマートフォン、タブレット端末において、無料でストリーミング再生することができます。下記 URL よりご利用ください。再生手順や動作環境などは本書巻末の「Web 動画のご案内」をご覧ください。

https://st.seibido.co.jp

音声ファイルのダウンロードについて

CD マークがある箇所は、ダウンロードすることも可能です。下記 URL の書籍詳細ページにあるダウンロードアイコンをクリックしてください。

https://www.seibido.co.jp/ad665

はじめに

　このテキストはアメリカの３大ネットワークのひとつであるCBSの看板ニュース報道番組"CBS Evening News"と朝の情報番組"CBS This Morning"、そしてその日曜版の"CBS Sunday Morning"の中で取り上げられたニュースを収録したものです。

　個性豊かなアンカーや記者たちが様々な話題についてレポートしているため、英語を外国語として学んでいる学習者にとってもたいへん興味深いものがありますが、本書はその中から特に日本人英語学習者にとって身近で親しみやすく、アメリカ人の生活や文化を直接反映しているニュースを厳選しました。今シリーズでは特に新型コロナによるパンデミックという厳しい状況の中、人と人との結びつきや多様な価値観の受け入れなど、社会における様々な問題にアメリカ人が日々の生活の中でどのように取り組んできたかについて取り上げています。また、現代日本の社会や事象が扱われている話題も含まれており、日本や日本文化が現在のアメリカ人にどのように受け止められているかを垣間見ることができます。

　IT技術の急速な進展のおかげで、本テキストのニュース素材がネットを通して、スマートフォンやコンピュータ上で簡単に視聴できるようになっています。ストリーミング形式での配信のため、手元の機器には保存することはできませんが、ネットにつながっていればいつでもどこからでも視聴することができます。学習する際には映像をヒントにしながら視聴しその内容を理解することが第１の目標となりますが、その内容を十分理解したあとでニュースの音声に合せて「シャドーイング」を行うことによって、英語の音声面の強化をはかることもめざしています。アンカーやレポーターたちは限られた時間内にできるだけ多くの情報を盛り込もうとしているため、１分間に150語から200語程度の速さで話しています。英語を外国語として学んでいる学習者がそれと同じように真似て復唱するのにはかなり無理がありますが、本テキストでは最新の話速変換技術を用いて、生の素材を生かしながらそのスピードを85％程度に遅くした音声や動画も併せて提供しています。ニュースに登場する人々の英語には生の感情がそのまま込められていますので、それをくりかえし練習することによってリスニング力を高めるとともに、英語特有の強弱のリズムやイントネーションをぜひ体感してください。また、各ユニットの最後にはニュースについて、「あなたはどう思いますか？あなたならどうしますか？」というように、話題を自分の立場に置き換えて考える活動が用意されています。多量のインプットに加えてこのように自分の考えをアウトプットすることによって、学習した言語項目を使いながら英語を身につけることができるようになっています。ニュースを理解するだけにとどまらず、様々な話題について自ら考え、それを英語で発信できる本物の英語力をぜひ身につけて下さい。

Nobuhiro Kumai & Stephen Timson

CONTENTS

75% WORK CANCELED, MOVED REMOTE OR DELAYED
SOURCE: COLLEGE REACTION/AXIOS POLL CORONAVIRUS APRIL 10-12

UNIT 1

Young Boy Seeks to Spread His Love of Literacy

YOUTH ACTIVISM / LITERACY

ⓢCBS EVENING NEWS WITH NORAH O'DONNELL

ⓢCBS EVENING NEWS WITH NORAH O'DONNELL

 1. Before You Watch

Look at the title and photos, and then answer the questions.

1. What do you think the title of this news story means?

2. Look at the sign in the photo above. Can you guess how the boy in the news story title is spreading his love of reading?

6

2. Word Match

Match each word or phrase with the right definition below.

(   ) **1.** Misaki has wanted to **make a difference** ever since she entered university and began learning about SDGs.

(   ) **2.** My local supermarket **gives away** reusable shopping bags instead of single-use plastic bags.

(   ) **3. Donation**s to charities are needed months or even years after a disaster strikes.

(   ) **4.** This government program is intended to promote adult **literacy** among people who have had very little education.

(   ) **5.** My university offers many scholarships every year to students **in need**.

(   ) **6.** Honesty is a **virtue** that teaches us not to lie, steal, or cheat.

(   ) **7.** My boss showed **compassion** when he allowed me to work at home so I could care for my sick mother.

(   ) **8.** The snowstorm started a **ripple effect** that caused many missed flight connections and cancellations.

---

a. to provide something for free

b. a situation where one event causes a series of other events to happen

c. a strong feeling of sympathy and sadness for the suffering or bad luck of others and a wish to help them

d. to do something that helps people, or makes the world a better place

e. a good moral quality in a person; morally good behavior or character

f. the ability to read and write

g. not having enough food, money, or support

h. something such as money, food, clothes, etc. that you give to a person or organization

---

 3. Getting the Gist (First Viewing) [Time 01:38] WEB動画

Watch the news and choose the right word for each statement.

1. Orion Jean's speech won a student kindness contest and it (excited / guided / inspired) him to share his love of literacy with others.

2. Orion Jean is (buying / collecting / reading) used books from people around the country and donating them to children in need.

4. Getting into Details (Second Viewing)

Watch or listen to the news again. Fill in the blanks and answer the questions.

[1-03]

Bill Whitaker: If you don't think one person can **make a** big **difference**, we know a young man who might just
₁(   ). CBS's Janet Shamlian introduces us.

5 **Janet Shamlian:** Getting books into the hands of children.

Orion Jean: Fresh shipment!

Shamlian: Hundreds of titles **given away** at this Fort Worth Book Fair ...

10 **Orion:** Well, we just got a **donation**, a generous donation of books.

Shamlian: ... by a child himself.

Orion: I want to be ₂(   ) my love of **literacy** with as many people as possible.

> **Fresh shipment!**
> （本が）新たに入荷
> したよ！
>
> **titles**
> 出版物、本
>
> **Fort Worth**
> 米国テキサス州の
> 都市
>
> **generous**
> 寛大な、気前のよい

Comprehension Check

1. **[T / F]** Donated books are given away for free to children at the Fort Worth Book Fair.
2. **[T / F]** Orion Jean wants to share his love of literacy with people who donate books.

[1-04]

15 **Shamlian:** This is Orion Jean. He's ten, but the number ₃(   ) is 500,000 — the number of books he's hoping to get donated to children **in need**.

Orion: Even just for a moment, to go into a new story or a new world, and go to ₄(   ) they never would have.

> **get donated**
> 寄付を受ける

Kindness is a **virtue** we can all possess, if we are willing
to. So why not start today? Because right now, it's $_5($
) more than ever.

25

| more than ever |
| かつてないほど |

3. **[T / F]** Orion's goal is to donate 500,000 books to children in need.
4. **[T / F]** Children can enter a new story or a new world by going to a book fair.
5. **[T / F]** Orion says that anyone can be kind if they are willing to try.

[🎧1-05]

Shamlian: That speech won Orion a 2020
student kindness contest,
inspiring his own personal
campaign of **compassion**.

inspiring ~
そして（それが）～
に刺激を与えた

30 *Orion:* The speech contest was really just the catalyst to something
$_6($).

catalyst
きっかけ、触媒とな
るもの

Shamlian: With 120,000 books collected so far, Orion is asking
people across the country to give away their used books
to $_7($).

35 *Orion:* They can give that book away to another child who may
need it, and it causes **ripple effect** [*sic*]. And ... that's what
it's all about.

that's what it's
all about
つまるところそうい
う（重要な）ことな
んです

Shamlian: $_8($) from a boy who has yet to start
the sixth grade. Janet Shamlian, CBS News, Fort Worth.

has yet to ~
まだ～していない

40 *Whitaker:* What a remarkable young man, doing remarkable things!

6. **[T / F]** Winning the speech contest motivated Orion to be kind to others, so he
started his own personal campaign of collecting and donating books to
children.
7. **[T / F]** Donating a used book to children in need has a ripple effect because others
will be motivated to give away their books too.
8. **[T / F]** The news reporter says that Orion has already started the sixth grade.

5. Summary

Fill in the blanks. The first letter of each word is already provided.

It is possible for one person to make a big ₁(**d**   ) in the lives of others through kindness. Orion Jean is only ten years old. He shares his love of ₂(**l**   ) by collecting and donating books to children in ₃(**n**   ). He believes ₄(**r**   ) books helps children enter a new world and meet people they would never meet. 5 Winning a student kindness speech contest was the ₅(**c**   ) that inspired his own personal campaign of compassion. He asked people across the country to donate their used books to children. Giving a book ₆(**a**   ) to another child who may need it causes a ₇(**r**   ) effect. So far, he has ₈(**c**   ) 120,000 books. 10 Hundreds of titles were given away at a book fair in Fort Worth, Texas. Orion has deep ₉(**t**   ) for a boy who has not ₁₀(**y**   ) started the sixth grade.

6. Retelling the News Story

Look at the photos below and fill in each blank with the letter of the appropriate answer. Then use the photos and sentences as a guide to retell the news story to your partner or group.

This news story is about Orion Jean, a ten-year-old boy who wants to ₁____ through kindness. He collects used books and donates them to ₂____. He thinks ₃____ can give them a whole new experience.

Orion won a speech ₄____ about kindness and it encouraged him to ask people to ₅____ their old books to children.

The boy thinks this small kindness will cause a ₆____ on others. The reporter thinks that Orion ₇____ for a ten-year-old boy.

a) reading books	b) create change	c) ripple effect	d) donate
e) contest	f) is a deep thinker	g) poor children	

7. In My Opinion

Write a few words about your opinion of this news story. Then share your opinion with your partner or group.

In my opinion, ...
....
....

8. Conversation in Action

 1-08

Put the Japanese statements into English. Then listen to check your answers.

Jake: Hey, Sara, what's up?

Sara: Oh, hi Jake. Look at all these old books! What'll I do!

Jake: Why ₁_____?
(困窮している子どもたちにそれらを寄付したらどうかな)

Sara: *Sounds great!* But how?

Jake: Um. You could start by asking a friend for an old book.
₂_____, you know.
(たとえ一人であっても大きな変化を生じさせることができるよ)

Sara: Oh, *I get it!* And then that friend could ask another friend, like a ripple effect.

Jake: Right! And then ₃_____.
(ブックフェアみたいなイベントでそれら全てを人にあげることができるよ)

Sara: *Sweet!* *By the way*, Jake, do you have any old books? Ha ha.

Word Help ***Sounds great! / Sounds good!**: used when you agree with something, or tell someone that their idea or suggestion seems like a good one *Example: "How about dinner and a movie tonight?" "Sounds great."*

*I get it: used when you want to say that you've understood something *Example: "Do you understand what I'm saying?" "I get it, thanks!"*

*Sweet: used to show that you are happy about something or think it is good *Example: "I passed my driving test!" "Sweet! Let's go for a drive!"*

*By the way (SNS:BTW): used to casually introduce or emphasize additional information in a conversation *Example: I'm glad you liked the movie. By the way, it won an Oscar for Best Picture.*

Conversation in Action CHALLENGE

Use the vocabulary and phrases you learned in this unit to make a short conversation with your partner. Then practice your conversation with your partner or group.

11

9. Critical Thinking

Discuss the following questions with your partner or group. Give reasons to support your opinions.

Understanding the News

1. What does the boy in the news story want to do?

2. What is he asking people to do?

3. How is he going to do this?

What Do You Think?

1. Do you like to read books? Why? / Why not?

2. What are some advantages and disadvantages of reading books on an electronic device (e.g., a smartphone or tablet) versus reading on paper?

3. Why is it important to be kind to others?

4. What is one thing you can do right now to make a difference in the lives of others?

UNIT 2

Graduation Day Surprise

INCLUSION / CHARITY

GRADUATION DAY SURPRISE

ⒸCBS EVENING NEWS WITH NORAH O'DONNELL

 1. Before You Watch

Look at the title and photos, and then answer the questions.

1. What usually happens at a high school graduation ceremony?

2. Can you guess what the surprise was at this graduation ceremony?

2. Word Match

Match each word or phrase with the right definition below.

(   ) **1.** That movie was a bummer, because the story was too **predictable**.

(   ) **2.** Japan is gradually opening its doors to more **immigrant**s due to the shrinking working-age population.

(   ) **3.** It's hard to succeed in this business, but if you work hard, you'll **make it** eventually.

(   ) **4.** I was able to get a college **scholarship** to study at a top university in the States.

(   ) **5.** I'm so **grateful for** all your help and support.

(   ) **6.** My family's **expenses** are constantly rising, but my income stays the same.

(   ) **7.** College graduates are having a real **struggle** to get a good job in this gig economy.

(   ) **8.** Having a **college degree** can certainly open many doors in your career.

---

a. money given to a student by a school or an organization, etc. to help pay for their education

b. the qualification students get when they successfully complete a university or college course of study

c. a person who comes to live permanently in a foreign country

d. the amount of money that is needed to pay for or buy something

e. being able to know in advance what will happen or what something will be

f. to be successful; to succeed in doing (something that you attempt)

g. a very difficult task that you can do only by making a great effort

h. feeling or showing thanks to someone for some helpful act

---

3. Getting the Gist (First Viewing) [Time 01:48]

WEB動画   DVD

Watch the news and choose the right word for each statement.

1. Verda Tetteh (earned / made / recovered) a standing ovation from the crowd at her graduation ceremony.

2. Verda's mother, Roseberry (announced / repeated / shouted) loudly when Verda said she was giving away her scholarship.

4. Getting into Details (Second Viewing)

WEB動画 🖥️ 📀 DVD 💿 CD 1-10~13

Watch or listen to the news again. Fill in the blanks and answer the questions.

[💿 1-10]

Norah O'Donnell: Graduation ceremonies are often **predictable**, but something remarkable happened when a student decided to go off script with

5　　　a ₁(   ).
Here's CBS's Nikki Battiste.

Verda Tetteh: At Fitchburg High, ...

Nikki Battiste: As the class speaker at her Massachusetts high school graduation, Verda Tetteh earned a ₂(   ).

10　*Verda:* To every **immigrant** child, you can **make it**.

| go off script |
| スピーチ原稿に書いてないことを話す |

| class speaker |
| クラス代表としてスピーチをする人 |

Comprehension Check

1. **[T / F]** Norah O'Donnell says that graduation ceremonies often follow a certain style or tradition.
2. **[T / F]** Nothing unusual or special happened at the graduation ceremony in the news report.
3. **[T / F]** The people in the audience stood up and cheered when they heard Verda's unselfish offer.

[💿 1-11]

Battiste: But it's what she did next that had the crowd in awe. After winning a $40,000 **scholarship**, ...

Verda: Sorry again for interrupting, ...

15　*Battiste:* ... the 17-year-old ₃(   ).

Verda: ... I am so very **grateful for** this. But I also know that I am not the one who needs this the most.

Battiste: Tetteh is heading to Harvard this fall on a full scholarship,
20　　　but she ₄(   ) the money for **expenses**.

| had ~ in awe |
| ～に畏敬の念を抱かせた |

| $40,000 scholarship |
| 彼女の高校から贈られた奨学金の額 |

| interrupting |
| 話を中断してしまって |

| full |
| 全額支給の |

4. [T / F] After winning the $40,000 scholarship, Verda gave it away.

5. [T / F] Verda was not grateful for winning the scholarship.

6. [T / F] Verda could have used the scholarship award from her high school to pay for her expenses at Harvard.

[🔊 1-12]

Battiste: What was it that made you think, "I wanna give $40,000 away"?

Verda: It just was a thought that there's ₅(   ) who might have a **struggle**, you know, like my mom did when she was going to community college.

25

community college
地域の短期大学

Battiste: Mom Rosemary, an immigrant from Ghana, got her community **college degree** when she was 47.

In that moment when Verda says, "I'm giving this money away," what was ₆(   )?

30 *Rosemary Tetteh:* I was just happy, I stood up and started shouting so loud. I was afraid those in front of me will be like, "Why is she that loud?" But I was so 35 happy with her decision.

will be like ～
〔～というようなことを〕言うんじゃないかって

Verda: You know, you don't have to have the world to be able to give anything, you know, you ... the little you have, just ₇(   ) around you and how you can 40 help.

the little you have
たとえ持っているものがどんなに少なくても

7. [T / F] Verda wanted to give the scholarship money to someone like her mother, Rosemary, who struggled when she was a college student.

8. [T / F] Verda's mother shouted happily when Verda said she was giving the scholarship away.

9. [T / F] Verda thinks that you have to be rich before you are able to give anything to help others around you.

[🎧 1-13]

Announcement: Verda ...

Battiste: Tetteh plans to study chemistry at Harvard. But it's clear she's already learned ₈(

). Nikki Battiste, CBS News, Fitchburg, Massachusetts.

45

O'Donnell: Looks like Verda is ready to take on the world.

take on the world
人生で起こる様々な
難題に立ち向かう

Comprehension Check

10. **[T / F]** Battiste says Verda has not started studying at Harvard yet, but she has already learned an important life lesson.
11. **[T / F]** O'Donnell thinks that Verda is not ready to succeed in the world.

5. Summary

 1-14

Fill in the blanks. The first letter of each word is already provided.

Graduation ceremonies are often ₁(**p**   ). But something remarkable happened at a high school graduation in Massachusetts. The class speaker, Verda Tetteh, won a $40,000 ₂(**s**   ), but ₃(**g**   ) it away. The audience gave her a standing ovation when they heard her surprising and selfless offer. Verda also told her classmates they could ₄(**m**   ) it. Although Verda was very₅(**g**   ) for the scholarship, she knew that there were other ₆(**i**   ) children who needed it more. She thought about her mother, Rosemary, who ₇(**s**   ) to get a community college ₈(**d**   ). Rosemary was very happy with her daughter's decision. Verda is heading to Harvard on a full ₉(**s**   ). So, she could have used the money for ₁₀(**e**   ). But she thinks it is important to think about others and help them. The reporter said Verda has not started studying at Harvard yet, but it's clear she has already learned what really ₁₁(**m**   ).

5

10

6. Retelling the News Story

Look at the photos below and fill in each blank with the letter of the appropriate answer. Then use the photos and sentences as a guide to retell the news story to your partner or group.

This news story is about Verda Tetteh, who ₁___ the crowd at her graduation ceremony by giving her $40,000 ₂___ away to another student who needed it more.

Verda's mother, Rosemary, is an immigrant from Ghana, and ₃___ to get her college degree. So Verda knows how important a good ₄___ is. Rosemary was very happy when she heard her daughter's selfless ₅___.

Verda says that even though you don't have much money, it is important to ₆___ about others around you and help them. She has already learned what is really ₇___.

a) struggled	b) surprised	c) education	d) important
e) offer	f) think	g) scholarship	

7. In My Opinion

Write a few words about your opinion of this news story. Then share your opinion with your partner or group.

In my opinion, ...

....

....

8. Conversation in Action

 1-16

Put the Japanese statements into English. Then listen to check your answers.

Jake: What are your plans after graduation, Sara?

Sara: I'm still deciding. How about you?

Jake: 1._____.
Even a full scholarship won't cover all my expenses.
（大学に行きたいな　でも金銭的にその余裕があるかわからないけど）

Sara: Well, why don't you go to a community college instead? It's a lot cheaper.

Jake: Hmm. Then I 2._____.
That's a great *plan B,* Sara. Thanks.
（そんなに苦労しなくてもいいかもしれないな）

Sara: *No biggie.* 3._____.
（よい教育を受けることは本当に大切なことよ）

Word Help *plan B: an alternate plan used when the original plan fails, or if things do not happen the way you expect
Example: It's too late to go to the movie. Let's do plan B and just have dinner instead.

*No biggie: used to say something is not a problem, difficult, or troublesome
Example: "Thanks for your help." "No biggie."

Conversation in Action CHALLENGE

Use the vocabulary and phrases you learned in this unit to make a short conversation with your partner. Then practice your conversation with your partner or group.

9. Critical Thinking

Discuss the following questions with your partner or group. Give reasons to support your opinions.

Understanding the News

1. What did Verda win at the graduation ceremony?
2. Why did the crowd give her a standing ovation?
3. Why did she do that?

What Do You Think?

1. Do you think you would make such a generous offer if you were in the same situation as Verda? Why? / Why not?
2. Do you think a college education is necessary to succeed in life? Why? / Why not?
3. What are some reasons people immigrate?
4. Have you ever thought of immigrating to another country? Why? / Why not? If yes, where would you go, and why?

UNIT 3

A Mission to Help the Homeless

®CBS EVENING NEWS with NORAH O'DONNELL

®CBS EVENING NEWS with NORAH O'DONNELL

 1. Before You Watch

Look at the title and photos, and then answer the questions.

1. What do the terms *mission* and *homeless* mean?

2. What do you think the little boy's mission is?

2. Word Match

Match each word or phrase with the right definition below.

( ) **1.** Children often **look to** their parents or teachers **for** advice and support.

( ) **2.** The experiment produced some **unexpected** results.

( ) **3.** She is a passionate **advocate** of fair trade between countries.

( ) **4.** She's always **hand**ing **out** advice to her co-workers.

( ) **5.** The new department is in charge of **expand**ing our business overseas, especially in Asian countries.

( ) **6.** Volunteer groups from around the world are providing food and other basic **essential**s to Ukrainian refugees.

( ) **7.** I can't believe my friends **got** me **to** audition for *America's Got Talent*. I don't think my dancing is good enough.

( ) **8.** There's no simple **solution** to poverty and homelessness.

---

a. something absolutely necessary or needed

b. surprising because you were not thinking it would happen

c. someone who strongly and publicly supports someone or an action

d. to make something greater in size, number, or importance

e. to hope that someone will provide something for you: to depend on someone

f. a way of finding an answer to a problem or dealing with a difficult situation

g. to give something to each person in a group or place

h. to persuade or make someone do something

---

3. Getting the Gist (First Viewing)   [Time 01:31]

Watch the news and choose the right word for each statement.

1. When the news reporter first met Begg, he was (buying / collecting / saving) shower caps, gloves, and masks from local hotels and giving them to staff that took care of him when he was in the hospital.

2. Now, Begg is handing out meals and other (equipment / essentials / pieces) donated by companies to the homeless, and families with sick children.

4. Getting into Details (Second Viewing)

 1-18~20

Watch or listen to the news again. Fill in the blanks and answer the questions.

[1-18]

Norah O'Donnell: Americans **look to** Washington **for** leadership, when we found it along with ₁(   ) from an **unexpected** source. Here is CBS's Kris Van Cleave.

5 *Kris Van Cleave:* In the shadow of a symbol of American accomplishment sits a park lined with tents that most in the nation's capital ₂(
10   ).

Sharon Wise: You got Chick-Fil-A tonight.

Van Cleave: But not eight-year-old Zohaib Begg. Along with homeless **advocate** Sharon Wise, the Virginia third grader is **hand**ing **out** ₃(   )
15 and care packages of socks, masks and toiletries.

a symbol of American accomplishment
ここでは画面に映っている Capitol Building（米国の国会議事堂）を指す

nation's capital
米国の首都である Washington D.C.

Chick-Fil-A
チキンサンドイッチ

care packages
救援物資

toiletries
洗面用具

Comprehension Check

1. [T / F] Americans depend on their government for leadership.
2. [T / F] The tents lining the park near the Capitol are symbols of American achievement.
3. [T / F] The news reporter said most people living in Washington D.C. ignore the homeless problem.
4. [T / F] Sharon Wise is homeless, and lives in the park where Zohaib Begg is handing out donated meals and other essentials.

[1-19]

Wise: It doesn't matter wh ... how old you are, you can help someone.

Van Cleave: So many people drive by these folks every day, and don't stop. What ₄(   )?

20 *Zohaib Begg:* Because they ... they don't really have ... have a lot of stuff like we do. So I really, ... so I really want to help them.

drive by ~
~のそばを車で通る

stop
（手助けするためにわざわざ）車を止める

23

Van Cleave: When we first met Begg last April, he was collecting shower caps, ₅(

) from local hotels for the hospital staff that saved him from a tumor when he was four.

How much stuff did you get?

Begg: 6,009 PPEs.

tumor
腫瘍

PPE
個人用防護具
（通常単数形）

Comprehension Check

5. [T / F] Wise says Begg is too young to help the homeless.

6. [T / F] Most people who drive by the park every day stop and help the homeless people living there.

7. [T / F] Begg wants to help the homeless because they don't have a lot of personal possessions and goods.

8. [T / F] Begg began helping people by collecting PPEs from hotels and giving them to the hospital staff that took care of him when he was sick.

[🔊 1-20]

Van Cleave: Now Zohaib, who ₆(   ) the chief kindness officer, is **expand**ing his efforts, and inspiring friends and neighbors to help too, filling bags of **essentials** for the homeless and families with ₇(   ) staying at DC's Ronald McDonald House – all of it – Begg **got** companies **to** donate.

Begg: You just have to ₈(   ) and find one **solution**.

Van Cleave: A big idea from a little boy, with an even bigger heart.

Man: Thank you.

Van Cleave: Kris Van Cleave, CBS News, Washington.

chief kindness officer
CEO (Chief Executive Officer) のもじり

DC's Ronald McDonald House
米国首都にある病気の子とその家族のための宿泊施設

Comprehension Check

9. [T / F] Begg's friends and neighbors are helping him to collect and give essentials to children's hospitals.

10. [T / F] Begg was able to get companies to donate essentials to the homeless and families with sick children staying at DC's Ronald McDonald House.

11. [T / F] The reporter thinks Begg has a big idea for a boy his age.

5. Summary

 1-21

Fill in the blanks. The first letter of each word is already provided.

Americans $_1$(**l**   ) to Washington for leadership. However, the homeless living in a park in the nation's capital are forgotten by most residents of the city. The reporter says eight-year-old Zohaib Begg is an $_2$(**u**   ) source of compassion and leadership. Begg and homeless $_3$(**a**   ) Sharon Wise are helping the homeless by $_4$(**h**   ) out donated meals and care packages of socks, masks, and toiletries. Wise says age doesn't $_5$(**m**   ), because everyone can help. Begg wants to help the homeless because they don't have a lot of stuff like most people do. He began helping people by collecting PPE from hotels and giving them to some hospital staff. Now Begg is $_6$(**e**   ) his efforts by getting donations from companies, and inspiring friends and neighbors to help by filling bags of $_7$(**e**   ) for the homeless and families with sick children. Begg said he was able to find a problem and find one $_8$(**s**   ). The reporter thinks Begg has a big idea, and is very kind for a boy his age.

Look at the photos below and fill in each blank with the letter of the appropriate answer. Then use the photos and sentences as a guide to retell the news story to your partner or group.

This is a news story about an eight-year-old boy who helps the ₁___ living in tents in a park in Washington D.C. while many others ignore them.

Along with a homeless ₂___, Zohaib Begg ₃___ out meals and care packages he collected from hotels, hospitals, and companies. He says that he is helping them because they don't have ₄___ other people have.

Begg is ₅___ his efforts, and inspires others to join him to give out ₆___ to the homeless and families with sick children. No one is too young to make a ₇___!

a) essentials   b) things   c) advocate
d) expanding   e) difference   f) homeless   g) hands

 7. In My Opinion

Write a few words about your opinion of this news story. Then share your opinion with your partner or group.

In my opinion, ...

....

....

8. Conversation in Action

 1-23

Put the Japanese statements into English. Then listen to check your answers.

Jake: *Whew!* One more bag, and we're done!

Sara: *Awesome!* We have about 50 Care Kits all together.

Jake: I hope that's ₁_____

_____. (ホームレスキャンプで配布するための生活必需品の数が十分だ)

Sara: *No worries*, Jake. Any ₂_____

_____. （どんな贈物でも、たとえそれがいくら小さくても、私たちが気遣っていることを示しているわ）

Jake: You're a great homeless advocate, Sara. Homelessness is a big problem in our city.

Sara: *For sure.* ₃_____.

But I think anyone can help. （みんな解決策を市の指導者たちに期待してる）

Word Help | *Whew:* used to express surprise, relief, or a feeling of being very hot or tired
Example: **Whew!** *I finished all my exams!*

Awesome: wonderful; very impressive; excellent
Example: "I passed the job interview!" "**Awesome!**"

No worries: (AusE) an informal way to say, "Don't worry."
Example: "Oh no, we missed the train!" "**No worries**, another one is coming soon."

For sure: without doubt; definitely true
Example: "Global warming is getting worse every year." "**For sure.**"

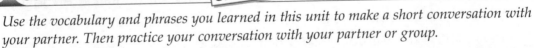

Conversation in Action CHALLENGE

Use the vocabulary and phrases you learned in this unit to make a short conversation with your partner. Then practice your conversation with your partner or group.

9. Critical Thinking

Discuss the following questions with your partner or group. Give reasons to support your opinions.

Understanding the News

1. Why does Begg want to help the homeless?

2. How did Begg first begin to help people?

3. What is Begg doing to expand his efforts to help the homeless and people in need?

4. What big idea does Begg have?

What Do You Think?

Homelessness is a global issue.

1. What are some of the most common reasons for homelessness?

2. How do you think the problem of homelessness can be solved?

3. Is your city or community experiencing homlessness? What are some causes and solutions for this problem?

Did you know?

American Accomplishment

米国首都ワシントン D.C. 市内で、政治の中枢部であるアメリカ国会議事堂 (U.S. Capitol Building) とホワイトハウス (White House) からポトマック川 (Potomac River) へと続く地域はナショナルモール＆メモリアルパーク (National Mall and Memorial Parks) と呼ばれ、約 405 ヘクタールにおよぶ緑地にリンカーン記念堂 (Lincoln Memorial) やワシントン記念塔 (Washington Monument) などアメリカを象徴する歴史的建造物や公園、広場がある。このニュースのリポーターは特にそこにある国会議事堂 (Capitol Building) を a symbol of American accomplishment と表現している。In the shadow of ～とは「政治の中心地であり、政治的指導者たちが多くいる国会議事堂の**陰が当たるくらい近くの所に**」という意味である。

UNIT 4

Fly Me to the Moon
— SpaceX to Fly Japanese Billionaire to Moon —

JAPAN / SPACE TOURISM

CBS THIS MORNING
FLY ME TO THE MOON
MUSK REVEALS BILLIONAIRE TOURIST FOR SPACEX TRIP

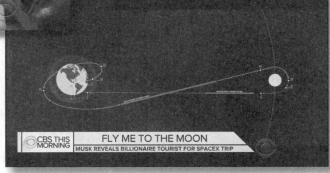

CBS THIS MORNING
FLY ME TO THE MOON
MUSK REVEALS BILLIONAIRE TOURIST FOR SPACEX TRIP

 1. Before You Watch

Look at the title and photos, and then answer the questions.

1. Who is Elon Musk, and what is SpaceX?

2. Do you know who the billionaire tourist in the photo is?

2. Word Match

Match each word or phrase with the right definition below.

(   ) **1.** Could you **book** a flight from Tokyo to Los Angeles for me?

(   ) **2.** He is the **founder** of a popular hamburger chain with restaurants all across California.

(   ) **3.** Scientists hope that data from the research will be useful for a more detailed **exploration** of Mars.

(   ) **4.** The new employee comes to every meeting, but he doesn't **contribute** much **to** the discussions.

(   ) **5.** China has more than one billion smartphone users, and nearly 90 percent of online shoppers have **purchase**d items via their mobile phones.

(   ) **6.** This stove is **equip**ped **with** a safety feature which automatically shuts it off when it gets too hot.

(   ) **7.** You are supposed to hand in your assignments by the **deadline**.

(   ) **8.** Any **investment** involves an element of risk.

---

a. to buy something

b. the action of traveling in or through an unfamiliar area in order to learn about it

c. the act of using money to make more money

d. a date or time when something must be done

e. to make arrangements for (someone) to do, use, or have something at a later time

f. to give something, especially money or goods, to help achieve something

g. a person who starts a school, organization, business, etc.

h. to provide a person, object, or place with the things that they need for a particular purpose.

---

3. Getting the Gist (First Viewing)   [Time 02:23]

Watch the news and choose the right word for each statement.

1. Billionaire Yusaku Maezawa paid CEO Elon Musk's company to (rent / repair / ride) Space X's new big Falcon Rocket on a trip to the Moon.

2. After returning to Earth, the eight artists going on the trip with Maezawa will (create / imagine / recommend) something that will inspire people.

4. Getting into Details (Second Viewing)

Watch or listen to the news again. Fill in the blanks and answer the questions.

[🔊1-25]

John Dickerson: Japanese billionaire [*sic*] is the first passenger to **book** a trip to the Moon on a SpaceX rocket. CEO Elon Musk joined Yusaku Maezawa at the company's California headquarters yesterday. Maezawa paid an undisclosed

5   amount to ride on SpaceX's new Big Falcon Rocket. Musk says the Moon Project will ₁(

)   and could be

10 ready as early as 2023. Mireya Villarreal spoke to the Japanese billionaire after the announcement.

headquarters
本社
undisclosed amount
未公開の額

Comprehension Check

1. **[T / F]** Japanese billionaire Yusaku Maezawa is the first passenger to reserve a flight to the Moon on SpaceX's new Big Falcon Rocket.
2. **[T / F]** Elon Musk met Maezawa at the SpaceX company's office in Tokyo, Japan.
3. **[T / F]** SpaceX's Moon Project might be ready by 2023.

[🔊1-26]

Yusaku Maezawa: I ₂(   ) to the Moon.

Mireya Villarreal: In front of a **packed house**, SpaceX **founder**,

15   Elon Musk, introduced his newest partner in space **exploration**, billionaire Yusaku Maezawa.

packed house
満員の聴衆

Maezawa: I thought about how I can ₃(   ) to the world, and how this can

20 **contribute to** world peace. This is my life-long dream.

Villarreal: The founder of Japan's largest retail website, Maezawa **purchase**d every seat on the trip and plans to bring ₄(   ) along for the ride.

retail website
ネットショッピングサイト
bring ~ along
〜を連れて行く

25 *Maezawa:* These artists will be asked to create something after they return to Earth. And these masterpieces will ... will inspire the dreamer within all of us.

Comprehension Check

4. [T / F] There were only a few people in the audience when Musk introduced Maezawa as his newest partner in space exploration.

5. [T / F] Maezawa chose to go to the Moon to express appreciation for his own success, and show how space exploration can contribute to world peace.

6. [T / F] Maezawa established the largest retail website in Japan.

7. [T / F] Half of the available seats on the rocket were bought by Maezawa.

8. [T / F] Eight artists will create masterpieces during the trip to the Moon.

[🎧 1-27]

Villarreal: The BFR rocket will be nearly 400 feet long and **equip**ped **with** a reusable booster rocket that will produce 200 tons
30 of thrust. The plan is to $_5($)
the Moon and back, a more than 475,000-mile journey, in about five days.

BFR rocket
Big **F**alcon **R**ocket

booster rocket
補助推進ロケット

thrust
推進力

Elon Musk: This is a dangerous mission. Yes ... But it's definitely dangerous.

35 *Maezawa:* I'm not afraid of [*sic*] at all.

Villarreal: You're not afraid at all?

Maezawa: No.

Villarreal: Why? How?

Maezawa: I trust the SpaceX team.

FLY ME TO THE MOON
VEALS BILLIONAIRE TOURIST FOR SPACEX TRIP

Comprehension Check

9. [T / F] The booster rocket for the BFR rocket can be used again.

10. [T / F] The journey from the Earth to the Moon and back will last about five days.

11. [T / F] Maezawa told the reporter that he is afraid because it is a dangerous mission.

[1-28]

40   *Villarreal:* But SpaceX has ₆(   ) **deadline**s. Its last rocket, the Falcon Heavy, had its first successful launch nearly five years later than expected.

            What ₇(   ) that you can actually meet that 2023 deadline?

ELON MUSK
SPACEX CEO

45   *Musk:* It's not 100 percent certain that we succeed in getting this to flight. But we're gonna do everything humanly possible to bring it to flight as fast as 50   we can. Um ... and ... ₈(   ) we can.

  Villarreal: It's a risky **investment** 42-year-old Maezawa is willing to make for a shot at a lunar legacy. For CBS This Morning, Mireya Villarreal in Hawthorn, California.

Falcon Heavy
2018年2月6日に初めて打ち上げられた宇宙飛行用の大型ロケット

launch
ロケットの打ち上げ、発射

bring it to flight
それを飛ばす

for a shot at ~
～への挑戦に対して

lunar legacy
（後世の人々に）月に行くというレガシーを残す事

Comprehension Check

12. [T / F] The Falcon Heavy, SpaceX's last rocket, was launched ahead of schedule.

13. [T / F] Musk is not completely sure his company can meet the 2023 deadline.

14. [T / F] The reporter thinks investing in the Moon project is risky, but Maezawa is willing to take a chance at achieving his dream and making history.

5. Summary

Fill in the blanks. The first letter of each word is already provided.

A Japanese billionaire is the first passenger to ₁(**b**   ) a trip to the Moon on a SpaceX rocket. SpaceX ₂(**f**   ) Elon Musk introduced Yusaku Maezawa as his newest partner in space ₃(**e**   ) at the company's California headquarters. Maezawa is the founder of Japan's largest retail website. He chose to go to the Moon to give back to the world, and ₄(**c**   ) to world peace. Maezawa ₅(**p**   ) every seat on the trip, and plans to bring up to eight artists along for the ride. The artists will create something after they return to Earth that will inspire the dreamer within all of us. SpaceX's BFR rocket is ₆(**e**   ) with a reusable booster rocket. The Moon Project is a dangerous mission and will cost five billion dollars. The plan is to send passengers around the Moon and back in about five days. Musk said SpaceX will do everything possible to meet the 2023 ₇(**d**   ). Maezawa is willing to make a risky ₈(**i**   ) for a shot at a lunar legacy.

5

10

6. Retelling the News Story

Look at the photos below and fill in each blank with the letter of the appropriate answer. Then use the photos and sentences as a guide to retell the news story to your partner or group.

This is a news story about Japanese billionaire Yusaku Maezawa, who ₁____ all the tickets on Elon Musk's SpaceX rocket to the Moon. Maezawa is planning to bring some ₂____ along for the journey. He says he wants to give back to the world and ₃__ to world peace.

This mission plans to send ₄__ around the Moon and back in five days. It costs a lot of money and seems very ₅__. The development of the space rocket is behind schedule.

The space trip appears to be a ₆__ investment, but Maezawa says he's not ₇__ . He wants to take a shot at a lunar legacy.

a) artists	b) passengers	c) purchased	d) risky
e) contribute	f) afraid	g) dangerous	

7. In My Opinion

Write a few words about your opinion of this news story. Then share your opinion with your partner or group.

In my opinion, ...
....
....

8. Conversation in Action

🔊 1-31

Put the Japanese statements into English. Then listen to check your answers.

Sara: Hey, Jake. ₁_____
_____? The deadline for the launch is 2023.
（月旅行を予約した日本の億万長者について聞いた）

Jake: Oh, you mean, Maezawa? Yeah, I want to go too, ha ha.

Sara: *You wish!* He said he wants to give back to the world, and contribute to world peace.

Jake: *I've heard* that he purchased seats for some artists, too. ₂_____
_____.
（彼らが創る最高傑作が僕たちの中にいる夢追い人に刺激を与えてくれるだろうね）

Sara: That's true, but ₃_____
_____! And ticket prices are unbelievable!
（それは億万長者にとってさえも危険な投資だわね）

Jake: *Yep. *Way too* expensive for you and me, but we can always dream!

Word Help ***You wish!**: used to tell someone that what they want to happen or be true will definitely not happen or become true   *Example: "I'm going to be famous one day." "**You wish!**"*

*****I've heard**: to be aware of, or know of the existence of someone or something
*Example: **I've heard** that you got a new job.*

*****Yep:** yes (informal)   *Example: "Ready to go?" "**Yep.**"*

*****Way too:** "Way" adds extra emphasis to "too (adjective)." It makes the meaning stronger.
*Example: I'm **way too** busy to go to the meeting tomorrow.*

Conversation in Action CHALLENGE

Use the vocabulary and phrases you learned in this unit to make a short conversation with your partner. Then practice your conversation with your partner or group.

9. Critical Thinking

Discuss the following questions with your partner or group. Give reasons to support your opinions.

Understanding the News

1. Why did Yusaku Maezawa book a trip to the Moon on a SpaceX rocket?

2. How long will it take to send passengers around the Moon and return to Earth?

3. Why did the reporter say Maezawa's plan to go to the Moon is a risky investment?

What Do You Think?

1. What is space tourism?

2. What are some advantages and disadvantages of space tourism?

3. Would you like to go on a space tour to the Moon? Why / Why not?

UNIT 5

A Man on the Bench by the Beach

LIFE / INTERPERSONAL RELATIONSHIPS

 1. Before You Watch

Look at the title and photos, and then answer the questions.

1. Can you guess why the people in the photos want to talk with the man on the bench?

2. What do you think they are talking about?

37

2. Word Match

Match each word or phrase with the right definition below.

( ) **1.** The President has lots of **confidant**s in his inner circle who give him advice and opinions about what actions to take.

( ) **2.** Early morning **regular**s were surprised to find the coffee shop closed.

( ) **3.** We sometimes hear **weird** noises coming from the bedroom closet.

( ) **4.** I wish you wouldn't be so **judgmental** about the way I dress.

( ) **5.** In conversations, **nod**ding is a sign that you're interested in what the speaker is saying.

( ) **6.** Disasters like war and famine have affected **mankind** throughout history.

( ) **7.** He said that he started cycling during the pandemic to **clear** his **head**.

( ) **8.** I'm asking for your advice before making my decision because I **value** your opinion.

---

a. a trusted person you can talk to about personal and private things

b. very strange or unusual and difficult to explain

c. tending to form opinions too quickly, especially when disapproving of someone or something

d. to think that somebody/something is important and worthwhile

e. to stop worrying or thinking about something

f. the whole of the human race, including both men and women

g. a person who purchases products or services from a person or business frequently

h. to move your head up and down to show agreement, understanding, etc.

---

 3. Getting the Gist (First Viewing)   [Time 02:23]   WEB動画 **DVD**

Watch the news and choose the right word for each statement.

1. Al Nixon is not a trained therapist, but he is a (careful / strict / trusted) confidant and counselor to people who ask him for advice.

2. Al is not (satisfied / serious / surprised) anymore about what people tell him, and he is never judgmental.

4. Getting into Details (Second Viewing)

WEB動画 📺 DVD CD 1-33~36

Watch or listen to the news again. Fill in the blanks and answer the questions.

[🎵 1-33]

Steve Hartman: In St. Petersburg, Florida, when the sun rises, Al Nixon sets ... for his impromptu therapy sessions.

Al Nixon: (To woman) How've you been?

Hartman: Are you surprised at $_1$(   )?

5 **Nixon:** Not anymore.

Hartman: Al isn't a trained therapist.

Nixon: (To woman) I've been concerned.

Hartman: He actually works for the City Water Department.

10 **Nixon:** He's dismissing you.

Woman: Yeah.

Al Nixon sets
始める　　the sun rises に合わせた表現 (the sun sets)
impromptu 即興の、準備なしの
City Water Department 市の水道局
dismissing 受けつけない・拒絶 している

Comprehension Check

1. [T / F] Al Nixon's therapy sessions begin early in the morning.
2. [T / F] Al is always surprised by what people tell him.
3. [T / F] Al has studied psychology and therapy, and works as a professional therapist.
4. [T / F] The woman does not agree with Al's opinion.

[🎵 1-34]

Hartman: But in these early morning hours, he's a trusted **confidant** and counselor to $_2$(   ).

Renee Rutstein: And I wrote to him and I said ...

15 **Hartman:** Renee Rutstein is a **regular**.

Rutstein: He knows everything about me.

Hartman: Did you feel **weird** sharing all your secrets to a guy on a bench?

Rutstein: No, because he'll never judge me, and he always shoots me straight.

Bernadette Dorsett Mills: He's not **judgmental**, and he takes you for who you are.

Hartman: Bernadette Dorsett Mills says she has never ₃(
) .

Dorsett Mills: He's like the guiding force.

shoots me straight
私に対して率直に話す

guiding force
よい方向に導いてくれる人

Comprehension Check

5. **[T / F]** Al is a trusted confidant and counselor to anyone who asks him for advice.
6. **[T / F]** Renee Rutstein often speaks with Al about her concerns.
7. **[T / F]** Renee thinks it's strange to share her secrets with Al.
8. **[T / F]** Bernadette Dorsett Mills says Al accepts her as she is and is not judgmental.

[🎧 1-35]

Hartman: At the same time, I don't hear you talking a lot.

Nixon: No.

Hartman: I just see a lot of **nod**ding ... like you're doing now.

Nixon: (Nodding) Uh ... hmm. Uh ... hmm.

Hartman: A lot of uh ... hmms.

Nixon: Listening is *the* ₄(
) all **mankind** needs to know how to do very well.

Uh ... hmm ... uh ... hmm.

Hartman: A skill he has clearly mastered.

Nixon: Uh ... hmm.

Hartman: When Al started coming here seven years ago, the therapy was for him. He needed a quiet

place to **clear** his **head**, and the last thing he wanted was to hear other people's problems. But then a woman he'd never met ... told him something he'll never forget.

Nixon: She said, "Every day I see you, I know everything's gonna
45 be OK." And that ₅( ) that when you speak to someone or you smile, you let them know, "I **value** you." And people pick that up.

pick that up
それがわかる

Dorsett Mills: When I walk by sometimes you know, I don't even get a chance to chat with him, because there are ₆(
50) in line.

walk by
そばを通りかかる

Comprehension Check

9. [T / F] Al speaks more than he listens during a therapy session.
10. [T / F] Al doesn't think listening is a very important skill for people to know.
11. [T / F] Al first came to the beach seven years ago because he needed a quiet place to think clearly and calmly.
12. [T / F] Al says that people notice and feel valued and appreciated when you smile or speak to them.
13. [T / F] Dorsett Mills says she sometimes doesn't have a chance to chat with Al because there are other people waiting in line to talk with him.

[🎧1-36]

Hartman: In appreciation for always being there, not long ago, Al's faithful put a plaque on his bench, "To a loving and loyal friend and a confidant to
55 many, forever and always."

AL
A LOVING AND LOYAL FRIEND AND A CONFIDANT TO MANY FOREVER AND ALWAYS

In appreciation for ~
~に感謝して

faithful
信奉者、ファン

plaque
記念の飾り版

loyal
誠実な、忠実な

Nixon: I teared up. That was ... uh ... that was powerful.

teared up
泣きそうになるくらい涙が出てきた

Hartman: How can such a simple plaque be that powerful?

Nixon: When you express to someone, "You ₇( ) ..."
60 *Hartman:* They gave you back ₈( ). Everyone needs an Al ... even Al.

an Al
アルのような人

Woman jogging: Have a great day!

41

Nixon: You, too, eh!

14. [T / F] Friends and supporters showed their appreciation to Al by honoring him with a special plaque on his bench.

15. [T / F] Al was disappointed to receive the plaque because he thought it was too simple.

16. [T / F] The reporter thinks most people would not need someone like Al to ask for advice.

5. Summary

 1-37

Fill in the blanks. The first letter of each word is already provided.

Are you looking for honest advice from a sympathetic person? Al Nixon is not a trained therapist, and he actually works for the City Water Department. But early in the morning, he sits on a bench by the beach and gives impromptu therapy sessions. He is a trusted ₁(**c**   ) and counselor to whoever passes by. ₂(**R**   ) don't think it's ₃(**w**   ) to share their   5 secrets with Al. They say he is never ₄(**j**   ), and is a straight shooter who takes you for who you are. Al listens more than he speaks. He says listening is one skill all ₅(**m**   ) needs to know how to do very well. Al started coming to the beach because he needed a quiet place to ₆(**c**   ) his head. He says that people need to know that they   10 ₇(**m**   ). They feel ₈(**v**   ) and appreciated when you smile or speak to them. Al's faithful put a plaque on his bench to show their appreciation. The reporter says everyone needs someone like Al.

6. Retelling the News Story

 1-38

Look at the photos below and fill in each blank with the letter of the appropriate answer.
Then use the photos and sentences as a guide to retell the news story to your partner or
group.

This news story is about a man ₁___ on a bench by the beach who gives ₂___ to whoever passes by. His name is Al. He's not a trained ₃___, but people like his honest advice.

While people are talking to him, he just ₄___ and often nods, and is never ₅___. He says listening is the most important skill in life.

He's loved by his confidants so much that they made a ₆___ to show appreciation to him. Al says that people need to know they ₇___ to others.

a) plaque	b) sitting	c) judgmental	d) therapist
e) matter	f) listens	g) advice	

7. In My Opinion

Write a few words about your opinion of this news story. Then share your opinion with
your partner or group.

In my opinion, ...
....
....

8. Conversation in Action **1-39**

Put the Japanese statements into English. Then listen to check your answers.

Jake: Hey, Sara, everyone says you seem **kinda* weird lately. Are you OK?

Sara: **Not really.* I **messed up* at my part-time job and almost **got fired*. So, yeah, I've been **feeling down*.

Jake: Just take a little time to 1_____
_____. I'm sure your boss values you and your work.
（きみの頭をすっきりさせて、全力を尽くし続ける）

Sara: 2_____, Jake.
（アドバイスと悩みを聞いてくれてありがとう）

Jake: Sure. That's what friends are for. And 3_____
_____.（きみは大事な存在だってことと、僕たちみんな
きみのことを大切に思っていることを忘れないでね）

Sara: Thanks. I needed that. You're a great friend and confidant.

Word Help **kinda*: kind of (BrE srota: sort of) : used to soften other words and phrases so that they do not sound too direct or exact
*Example: "I was **kinda** sorry to see him go." "He looked **kinda** angry."*

*Not really: used to say "no" in a way that is not very forceful or definite
*Example: "Do you want to go to a movie?" "**Not really.**"*

*mess up: to make a mistake
*Example: I **messed up** and took the express instead of the local train.*

*got fired (BrE: sacked): to be dismissed from a job
*Example: He **got fired / sacked** because he came late to work many times for no reason.*

*feeling down: to feel sad, dejected, or depressed
*Example: He's been **feeling down** ever since he broke up with his girlfriend.*

 Conversation in Action CHALLENGE

Use the vocabulary and phrases you learned in this unit to make a short conversation with your partner. Then practice your conversation with your partner or group.

9. Critical Thinking

Discuss the following questions with your partner or group. Give reasons to support your opinions.

Understanding the News

1. Why don't people think it's weird to tell Al their secrets?

2. What skill does Al think is the most important for everyone to do well?

3. How did Al's faithful show their appreciation to him?

What Do You Think?

1. Which skill is more important when giving someone advice: listening or speaking? Why?

2. What do you do when you have a serious problem? What are some advantages and/or disadvantages of your problem-solving style?

3. How do you change your mood when you are feeling down?

4. Imagine you could write a letter to your younger self. What advice would you give to yourself?

UNIT 6
COVID Vaccine Inequalities

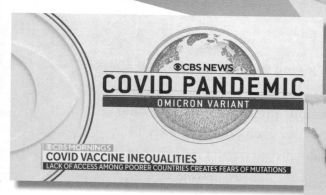

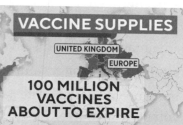

1. Before You Watch

Look at the title and photos, and then answer the questions.

1. What is a vaccine?

2. What do you think the terms, *vaccine inequality* and *variant* mean?

2. Word Match

Match each word or phrase with the right definition below.

(   ) **1.** Scientists and health experts say the new **variant** is likely to spread quickly and easily.

(   ) **2.** Since COVID-19 was first detected, the number of people **reinfect**ed with the coronavirus has been rising sharply.

(   ) **3.** The bad weather may have **account**ed **for** the small crowd.

(   ) **4.** The **vaccine**s scientists have developed are expected to protect against severe illness and hospitalization.

(   ) **5.** It's difficult to **predict** which team will come out on top.

(   ) **6.** The police officer pointed out my driver's license had already **expire**d.

(   ) **7.** The goods have been sitting in a warehouse for months because a strike has prevented **distribution**.

(   ) **8.** The country was plunged into economic **chaos** by the war.

---

a. the system of giving something out to people

b. to come to an end or to no longer be valid after a period of time

c. a substance that is injected into the body to stimulate the body's immune response against a disease

d. to become ill again after recovering from a previous illness caused by the same disease

e. a condition or place of great disorder or confusion

f. to give a reason or explanation for the cause of something

g. something that differs from others of the same kind or from a standard

h. to say that something will happen in the future

---

3. Getting the Gist (First Viewing)   [Time 02:52]   WEB動画 🖥 DVD

Watch the news and choose the right word for each statement.

1. Health experts say that unless there is global vaccine equity, the Omicron variant will (continue / start / stop) to change.

2. Many African countries do not have the necessary organizational and management capabilities to vaccinate people, and travel bans only further (isolate / protect / surround) this region.

Watch or listen to the news again. Fill in the blanks and answer the questions.

[CD 1-41]

Michelle Miller: We are learning more now about the Omicron **variant** from scientists in South Africa where it was

5 ₁( ).
An early study there found Omicron is at least 2.4 times more likely to **reinfect** someone who had COVID before, compared to other variants. The strain is also highlighting inequalities 10 in the global COVID response. Debora Patta is in Johannesburg. Debora, good morning.

strain
ウイルスの株

highlighting
浮き彫りにしている

response
対応

> **Comprehension Check**
>
> 1. [T / F] The Omicron virus was first reported by scientists in South Africa.
> 2. [T / F] Compared to other variants, Omicron does not reinfect people who already had COVID.
> 3. [T / F] The Omicron variant is focusing more attention on inequalities in how the world responds to COVID.

[CD 1-42]

Debora Patta: Good morning. In the turf war between Omicron and Delta, the new variant was 15 clearly winning, **account**ing **for** a meteoric rise in new infections in South Africa.

And it's inserted itself firmly into the global debate on 2( ). It's been the war cry of 20 health experts around the globe since the pandemic began — nobody is safe until everyone is safe.

Dr. Ayoade Alakija: Had we done the scientific thing, had we done what the scientists were saying, in January, February, 2020, we would not be now ₃( ).

turf war
縄張り争い

meteoric rise
急速な上昇

inserted itself~
~に加わった

war cry
ある理念に対する支持を集めるために用いられるスローガン

Comprehension Check

4. [T / F] The new Omicron variant is becoming more common than Delta, and is causing more infections.

5. [T / F] The increasing number of virus infections in South Africa has highlighted the problem of equal access to the COVID vaccines.

6. [T / F] Health experts were not aware of how unequal global access to vaccines would affect countries around the world when the pandemic began in 2020.

7. [T / F] Dr. Ayoade Alakija says the problem of some countries not having equal access to vaccines happened because people listened to the experts' and scientists' warning about vaccine inequality when the pandemic began in 2020.

[🎧 1-43]

25 *Patta:* And what science tells us, says a furious Dr. Ayoade Alakija, is that unless there is global **vaccine** equity, the virus will continue to mutate.

furious
憤慨した
equity
公平なこと
mutate
変異する

In the two countries where Omicron was first identified, Botswana has already administered 86 percent of its
30 supply, South Africa 78 percent. Compare this to $_4$( ), where it's predicted 100 million expired vaccines could be destroyed at the end of the year. This
35 is because they've hoarded them, says Alakija.

administered
実施した

hoarded
買いだめした

Dr. Alakija: We're saying "get out of the queue" so that we can get to the front of the line and get our own. And pay for them.

get out of the queue
並んでいる列から
離れる

Comprehension Check

8. [T / F] Dr. Alakija is very angry because scientific data shows that unless there is global vaccine equity, the virus will continue to mutate.

9. [T / F] Botswana and South Africa have administered less than 50 percent of their vaccine supplies.

10. [T / F] Wealthy nations hoard their vaccines because they expire too quickly.

11. [T / F] Dr. Alakija says wealthy nations should stop hoarding vaccines so that more vaccines are available to poorer countries.

Patta: Complicating matters further is **distribution**. Many African
40   countries lack the logistical capability to get shots into
people's arms and travel bans only further isolate this
region. Californian Monika Glass was visiting her
husband's family in South Africa when her flights were
canceled.

45 **Monika Glass:** Southern Africa is the only
place, who ... they instill [*sic*]
these travel bans, right, and I
just ... I feel like ₅(

). It's not right.

50 **Patta:** Then another blow. While waiting to make new travel
arrangements, she tested positive for COVID, and is
isolating in Cape Town.

Glass: I ... I have got mild symptoms. I am vaccinated, and I'm a
nurse, so I work in a COVID unit ... have been around
55   COVID. And this is the first that I've had COVID as far
as I'm aware.

Patta: Her far bigger concern is ₆(   ) to her
three children when the infection clears.

     Travel bans are causing further **chaos** with South African
60   scientists, saying there're fewer planes coming in that
can bring the necessary compounds to study Omicron,
sparking fears they could run out.

logistical capability 物流の能力

get shots into~ ～に注射を打つ

travel bans 渡航禁止令

isolate this region その地域を孤立させる

instill install（～を導入する）となるべき

blow 打撃
tested positive 検査で陽性と出た

have got mild symptoms 症状が穏やかだ
unit 部署

clears 消えてなくなる
compounds 化合物
sparking fears they could run out それらが底をつくことになるかもしれないという恐怖に拍車をかけている

Comprehension Check

12. **[T / F]** Distribution is another problem in fighting the virus, because many African countries do not have the logistical capability to vaccinate people.
13. **[T / F]** Monika Glass says the travel bans are helpful because they prevent people from traveling to southern Africa.
14. **[T / F]** Monika is more worried about getting back home to her children in California than she is about testing positive for COVID.
15. **[T / F]** Because flights are canceled, travel bans isolate a region, and that makes it difficult to bring in the necessary compounds to study the virus.

5. Summary

 1-45

Fill in the blanks. The first letter of each word is already provided.

Scientists are learning more about the Omicron $_1$(**v**   ), which was first reported in South Africa. An early study found that Omicron is at least 2.4 times more likely to $_2$(**r**   ) someone who had COVID before. Compared to the Delta strain, Omicron is becoming more common, $_3$(**a**   ) for a meteoric rise in new infections in South Africa, and highlighting the problem of   5
$_4$(**v**   ) inequality in the global COVID response. Dr. Ayoade Alakija is furious, because if the world had done $_5$(**w**   ) the scientists were saying in 2020, South Africa would not be in the situation it is now. She says that unless there is global vaccine equity, the virus will continue to mutate. Wealthy nations hoard vaccines that will soon $_6$(**e**   ) and be destroyed. Complicating   10
matters further is $_7$(**d**   ). Many African countries lack the logistical capability to vaccinate people. Travel bans cause $_8$(**c**   ) with family visits to South African relatives, and further isolate this region because planes cannot bring in the necessary compounds to study Omicron.

6. Retelling the News Story

 1-46

Look at the photos below and fill in each blank with the letter of the appropriate answer. Then use the photos and sentences as a guide to retell the news story to your partner or group.

This is a news story about a new $_1$____ of the coronavirus highlighting vaccine $_2$____ .

Dr. Ayoade Alakija says that if we had $_3$___ what scientists were saying in spring 2020, the situation would be $_4$___. The vaccine inequity can clearly be seen in $_5$___ countries in Africa. $_6$___ is another issue.

Travel bans are causing chaos because people cannot travel freely. It also $_7$___ the region because planes cannot bring in necessary materials to study Omicron.

a) done	b) distribution	c) variant	d) inequalities
e) different	f) poorer	g) isolates	

7. In My Opinion

Write a few words about your opinion of this news story. Then share your opinion with your partner or group.

In my opinion, ...
....
....

8. Conversation in Action 🎧 1-47

Put the Japanese statements into English. Then listen to check your answers.

Jake: Hi Sara. *If you don't mind me asking, ₁_____
_____? (ワクチン接種を受けるの？)

Sara: I already did, Jake. The new variants are more *contagious. And infections are rising again. How about you?

Jake: I'm *getting my shot tomorrow. Some COVID *mandates and travel bans have expired, so ₂_____ in
*cases. (それがいくつかの症例の上昇の説明にもなるね)

Sara: I guess everyone must be totally *worn out by all the chaos, and eager to reconnect with family and friends.

Jake: Yeah, but scientists say the virus will continue to mutate, so we still have to be careful.

Sara: Uh-huh. ₃_____.
I hope things get back to normal soon. (ワクチン接種を受けることはあなた自身だけでなくあなたの愛する人たちも守ることになるからね)

Word Help ***If you don't mind me / my asking:** used with a question as a polite way of asking something that could annoy, offend, or embarrass someone
*Example: **If you don't mind me asking**, how old are you?*

*contagious: a disease that can be spread from one person or organism to another by direct or indirect contact
*Example: People who have a **contagious** disease should be isolated.*

*get a shot (BrE jab): to receive an injection of a drug or medicine
*Example: My sister scheduled an appointment to **get a** COVID booster **shot**.*

*mandate: an official order to do something
*Example: Mask and vaccine **mandate**s help to prevent COVID infections.*

*case: an instance or occurrence, of a disease
*Example: Global COVID-19 **case**s continue to rise.*

*worn out: extremely tired or exhausted
*Example: He was **worn out** after the long flight from London*

Conversation in Action CHALLENGE

Use the vocabulary and phrases you learned in this unit to make a short conversation with your partner. Then practice your conversation with your partner or group.

9. Critical Thinking

Discuss the following questions with your partner or group. Give reasons to support your opinions.

Understanding the News

1. What does Dr. Alakija say is the reason for vaccine inequality?
2. What does she say will happen if the vaccine inequality continues?
3. What does she want wealthy nations to do to help solve this problem?
4. What other complications affect vaccine distribution in African countries?

What Do You Think?

1. Do you think the distribution of COVID-19 vaccines in Japan or your country is timely and efficient? Why?/Why not? Could it be improved? If so, how?
2. Do you think getting vaccinated is a personal choice, or a responsibility that everyone has to protect the health of others?
3. Give some examples of government mandates or measures that try to prevent and reduce COVID-19 infections in Japan or your country.
4. Do you think governments mandates or measures are necessary to keep people safe, or limit personal liberties and civil and economic freedoms?

UNIT 7

Surfing in Japan

JAPAN / SPORT

Kugenuma Folklore Museum

1. Before You Watch

Look at the title and photos, and then answer the questions.

1. Is surfing popular in Japan?

2. When do you think surfing started in Japan?

2. Word Match

Match each word or phrase with the right definition below.

(   ) **1.** Let's **grab** a bite to eat before the show starts.

(   ) **2.** I think I'm a smartphone **addict**. I can't seem to live without it.

(   ) **3.** I'm **hooked** on camping all by myself in the mountains.

(   ) **4.** Watching *Squid Game*, and other Korean TV dramas on Netflix has become my new **obsession**.

(   ) **5.** That part of the city has been **thriving** because the Olympic Games were held there.

(   ) **6.** This beautiful Japanese lacquer-ware was crafted by local **artisan**s in Kyoto.

(   ) **7.** The new line of products is carefully designed to **cater to** the needs of our target market.

(   ) **8.** You must **submit** your assignment by the end of the week.

---

a. continuing to be successful, strong, healthy, etc.

b. to get something to eat, but to do it quickly, because you don't have a lot of time

c. to give a document, proposal, report, etc. to somebody in authority so that they can make a decision about it

d. a person who is unable to stop using or doing something as a habit, especially something harmful

e. to satisfy a need, or to provide what is wanted or needed by a particular person or group

f. enjoying something so much that you want to do it, see it, etc. as much as possible

g. a person who does skilled work with their hands

h. the state in which a person's mind is completely filled with thoughts of one particular thing, or person in a way that is not reasonable or normal

---

 ## 3. Getting the Gist (First Viewing) [Time 03:06]

Watch the news and choose the right word for each statement.

1. Surfing made its (debut / performance / premiere) as an Olympic event at the 2020 Japan Olympics.

2. Surfing is one of the world's oldest sports, and it has been (gaining / maintaining / regaining) popularity in Japan since the end of World War II.

Watch or listen to the news again. Fill in the blanks and answer the questions.

[1-49]

Dana Jacobson: Tomorrow surfing makes its debut as an Olympic event. It's one of the world's oldest sports and as Lucy Craft reports, it's been ₁( ) in the host nation of Japan.

5　*Lucy Craft:* They arrive lugging boards on foot, or on two wheels. Among the estimated two million Japanese who ride waves, many crowd in here, one of the most beloved surf spots in the country.

10　It's only a little after 7 am, but we're well into rush hour down here at Kugenuma Beach. Some of these boards have been in the water since 4 am. While the rest of Japan is grabbing a coffee on their way to work, these

15　surfers have been ₂( ).

Masaya Uchida (voiceover): It's really laid-back here, and welcoming. It's like being in California.

Glossary
lugging (重くてかさばるものを)苦労して運びながら
estimated ~ およそ~
beloved 愛されている
we're well into ~ かなり~になっている
laid-back のんびりした **welcoming** 心地良い、友好的な
planks (木製の) 厚板

Comprehension Check

1. [T / F]　Surfing is one of the oldest Olympic sports.
2. [T / F]　Surfing is becoming more popular in Japan.
3. [T / F]　Kugenuma Beach is one of the most popular places to surf in Japan.
4. [T / F]　Kugenuma Beach is not very crowded in the morning.
5. [T / F]　Kugenuma Beach is very relaxing and friendly, so surfers feel like they are in California.

[1-50]

Craft: The Shonan coastline is so close to downtown Tokyo, surfing addicts can grab a few waves ₃( ).

20　Japanese have been body surfing for over a century, floating on small wooden planks, called *itago*, often decorated with ads for stores or soap.

But after World War II, when American soldiers in Japan began riding their long boards, Japanese were instantly **hooked**, said Tokyo author and surfer Kaori Shoji.

25

Kaori Shoji: They looked at the GIs having fun with just a board and they thought to themselves, "Hey, if they can do that, so

can we" and um, that's ... that's ₄(

30

). It's a place to have fun and relax and catch a wave or two, and uh, I think that was really seductive to the Japanese.

GIs
米軍兵士

thought to themselves
心の中で思った

seductive to ~
〜にとって魅力が
ある

Comprehension Check

6. [T / F] People living in Tokyo who want to surf on the Shonan coast can only go there on weekends because it is so far away.

7. [T / F] Japanese learned how to body surf from American soldiers.

8. [T / F] Japanese watching the GIs surf and having fun with long boards thought they could do the same, and became immediately hooked on surfing.

[🎧 1-51]

35

Craft: Japan's surfing **obsession** supports a **thriving** ₅(

) from the cafes and surf shops of seashore mecca, Chigasaki to a cottage industry of **artisan**s. Soeda Surfboard **cater**s **to** a notoriously finicky clientele. Boards

40

are fine-tuned to the surfer's skill level, body size, and local wave conditions. The semi-finished polyurethane blanks are sanded by hand, before getting a fiberglass

45

skin.

And over at Deuce Wetsuits, artisan Hiroshi Fukuzawa requires customers to **submit** a checklist of detailed body measurements, and pay nearly ₆(   ) as off-the-rack wetsuits.

mecca
人々が特定の目的を
もって集まる場所

cottage industry
家内工業

**notoriously
finicky clientele**
好みがうるさいこと
で悪名高い常連客

**polyurethane
blanks**
ポリウレタン製の発
泡フォームでできた
ボード

sanded
ヤスリをかけられる

skin
薄い膜

off-the-rack
既製品の

50

Hiroshi Fukuzawa (voiceover): Custom wetsuits were originally

handcrafted for Japanese ₇( ).
Then artisans **branched out into** wetsuits for surfers.

> **branched out into ~**
> ～にまで手を広げた

Comprehension Check

9. **[T / F]** Japanese obsessed with surfing support a growing and healthy beach culture that includes cafes, surf shops, and artisans.
10. **[T / F]** Surf gear is designed and made according to individual customer's requirements, such as skill level, wave conditions, and body size.
11. **[T / F]** Artisans first made wetsuits for Japanese pearl divers, and then started making them for surfers.

[🎧 1-52]

Craft: Japan's gentle waves are just right for **total newbies**.

Gary Burkhalter: I saw this perfect little **wave break**.

55 *Craft:* California **transplant** and now local surf instructor, Gary Burkhalter, showed me how to stay on my board ... **more or less**.

Burkhalter: You can surf in Hawaii, you can surf in California, you could surf, you know, anywhere in ... in Bali or somewhere, but surfing in Japan is like, wow, that's really special.

60

Craft: **Hot-dog** surfers must **bide their time**, ₈( ) to **churn up** the big waves. But **for the sheer joy of watery communion**, Japan's **surfin' safari** is a real **day at the beach**.

65

For CBS This Morning Saturday, Lucy Craft on the Shonan Coast, Japan.

total newbies
全くの初心者たち

wave break
波が砕ける

transplant
移住者

more or less
辛うじて、まあなんとか

Hot-dog
離れ業をする

bide their time
チャンスが来るのを待つ

churn up
激しく大量に次々と生み出す

for the sheer joy of watery communion
海岸での交流を純粋に楽しむためには

surfin' safari
もともとはサーファーが未知なる波を探し求めて旅に出ることを指す

day at the beach
海岸でのリラックスした楽しい時間

Comprehension Check

12. **[T / F]** The waves along Japan's coastline are too dangerous for beginner surfers.
13. **[T / F]** Gary Burkhalter is a surf instructor in California.
14. **[T / F]** More advanced and pro surfers have to wait patiently for bigger waves that are created by typhoons.

5. Summary

Fill in the blanks. The first letter of each word is already provided.

Surfing is one of the world's oldest sports, and made its Olympic debut at the Tokyo 2020 Summer Olympics. Surfing is gaining ₁(**p**   ) in Japan. The Shonan coastline is close to downtown Tokyo, so surfing ₂(**a**   ) can grab a few waves on the way to work. Japanese have been body surfing for over a century, floating on small wooden planks called *itago*. But after World War II, watching American soldiers having fun with just a board was really seductive and Japanese were instantly ₃(**h**   ). Japan's surfing ₄(**o**   ) supports a ₅(**t**   ) local beach culture, from cafes and surf shops to a cottage industry of ₆(**a**   ). Surf gear artisans ₇(**c**   ) to a finicky clientele. One wet suit shop requires customers to ₈(**s**   ) a checklist of detailed body measurements. Japan's gentle waves are just right for total newbies. But hot-dog surfers must wait for typhoons to churn up the big waves. For the sheer joy of watery fellowship, surfing in Japan is a real day at the beach.

 6. Retelling the News Story 🔊 1-54

Look at the photos below and fill in each blank with the letter of the appropriate answer. Then use the photos and sentences as a guide to retell the news story to your partner or group.

This news story is about surfing in Japan. The Shonan coastline is ₁____ to downtown Tokyo, so many surfers go there and enjoy ₂____ a few waves from early in the morning.

Japanese began body surfing with small wooden ₃____ over a ₄____ ago. They became ₅____ on surfing after World War II, when they saw American soldiers having fun with their long boards.

Japan's surfing ₆____ supports local surf culture from cafes and shops to surfboard and wet suit ₇____. Surfers in Japan really enjoy riding waves on the Shonan coast.

a) catching   b) artisans   c) obsession   d) hooked
e) century   f) planks   g) close

7. In My Opinion

Write a few words about your opinion of this news story. Then share your opinion with your partner or group.

In my opinion, ...

....

....

8. Conversation in Action

Put the Japanese statements into English. Then listen to check your answers.

Jake: *Yo, Sara, grab your board! *Surf's up!*

Sara: *Yay! The sun is shining, the *surf is heavy, and the weekend is here. *Dude, I am *stoked!*

Jake: *Whoa! ₁_____, ha!
（そんなに君がサーフィン狂だったなんて知らなかったよ）

Sara: Oh, yeah. My hometown is near the beach, so I got hooked when I was *like, twelve. Surfing is *kind of an obsession!

Jake: Wow, maybe you can help me get some surf gear.

Sara: Sure. ₂_____.
（ここには素敵なカフェやサーフショップがいくつかあるわよ） And ₃_____
_____. I'm sure we can find you some stuff. （初心者にあわせて作ってくれる職人さんも何人か知ってるわ）

Jake: Awesome!

Sara: Let's go catch some waves!

Word Help *Yo: informal word for "hello," used either as a greeting or to get someone's attention
Example: ***Yo,*** *It's 8:00! Time to get up!*

*Surf's up: the wave conditions are ideal for surfing *Example:* ***Surf's up!*** *Let's go catch some waves!*

*Yay: used to show happiness, approval, or excitement   *Example:* ***Yay!*** *I won a free trip to New York!*

*surf is heavy: large waves breaking on or near the shore   *Example:* *Today is very windy, so
the* ***surf is heavy.***

*Dude: slang term for a man; a guy *Example:* *Yo,* ***dude!*** *What's up?*

*stoked: extremely happy, excited *Example:* *I was so* ***stoked*** *about getting the job I couldn't sleep.*

*Whoa: used to express surprise, interest, or alarm, or to command attention *Example:* ***Whoa!***
You're really good at gaming!

*like: used informally as a filler word in a conversation to show uncertainty or that something
is approximate *Example:* *The new shopping mall is* ***like,*** *20 minutes away by train.*

*kind of: somewhat, or to a small degree *Example:* *It's* ***kind of*** *late. Let's do it tomorrow.*

60

Conversation in Action CHALLENGE

Use the vocabulary and phrases you learned in this unit to make a short conversation with your partner. Then practice your conversation with your partner or group.

9. Critical Thinking

Discuss the following questions with your partner or group. Give reasons to support your opinions.

Understanding the News

1. Why is Kugenuma Beach so popular with Japanese surfers?
2. When and how did surfing start in Japan?
3. Give some examples of how Japan's surfing obsession supports the local beach culture.

What Do You Think?

1. Why do you think surfing is gaining popularity in Japan?
2. Have you ever tried surfing? If yes, how did you like it? If not, would you like to try it? Why? / Why not?
3. Prepare a short report about a popular sport in Japan and make a presentation to your group or class. Describe it, and include information about how the sport started in Japan, and why it is popular.

UNIT 8

A New Beat
— High School Students Learn the Music Business —

A NEW BEAT
PHILADELPHIA TEENAGERS PRODUCE MUSIC WITH OWN RECORD LABEL

A NEW BEAT
PHILADELPHIA TEENAGERS PRODUCE MUSIC WITH OWN RECORD LABEL

 1. Before You Watch

Look at the title and photos, and then answer the questions.

1. What does, *A New Beat* mean?

2. What do you think these students are learning about the music business?

2. Word Match

Match each word or phrase with the right definition below.

(   ) **1.** You can hear some amazing **beat**s on the streets of New Orleans during Mardi Gras.

(   ) **2.** You may want to do an internship to gain **practical** experience and get an idea about where to work in the future.

(   ) **3.** Money and **fame** mean nothing if you are not happy.

(   ) **4.** It's important to find your **passion** and follow it.

(   ) **5.** Because you are so talented, you should **pursue** a career in music.

(   ) **6.** You need to be firm with her, or she'll try to **take advantage of** you.

(   ) **7.** The new intercultural training program will help diverse teams in our company **collaborate** better **with** each other.

(   ) **8.** He's a world-class striker who just landed a five-year **contract**, making him the highest-paid player ever.

---

a. to try to attain or accomplish (a goal) over a long period of time

b. the state of being known or recognized by many people because of your achievements, skills, talents, etc.

c. to work with another person or group in order to achieve something

d. relating to experience, real situations, or actions rather than ideas or imagination

e. to make use of somebody/something in a way that is unfair or dishonest

f. a musical unit of time that creates rhythm in a song or a piece of music

g. a legal document that states and explains a formal agreement between two different people or groups, companies, etc.

h. a very strong belief or feeling about something

---

3. Getting the Gist (First Viewing)   [Time 03:18]

Watch the news and choose the right word for each statement.

1. The Philadelphia School District has started a new music education program to make arts education more (possible / practical / probable).

2. Professional music producer Andy Hurwitz, who volunteers with the new program, (demanded / requested / suggested) the students start their own record label.

Watch or listen to the news again. Fill in the blanks and answer the questions.

[🎧 1-57]

Anthony Mason: Those are some of the latest **beat**s from the streets of

    Philadelphia, where a group of budding artists decided

    to start their own record label while still ₁(

). It's part of a new **push** by the city's

5   School District to make arts

    education more **practical**.

    Christina Ruffini caught up

    with the high school friends

    as they ₂(   )

10   release their latest single.

A NEW BEAT
PHILADELPHIA TEENAGERS PRODUCE MUSIC WITH OWN RECORD LABEL

Christina Ruffini: They don't yet have the **fame**, and the group doesn't

    actually have a name. But these Philly teens do have a

    record label and a producer, 18-year-old Caleb Autry.

budding artists
新進気鋭のアーティ
ストたち

record label
音楽会社

push
後押し

**city's School
District**
市の学区

caught up with~
～と会って(近況に
ついて)話した

Philly
フィラデルフィア市
の愛称

Comprehension Check

1. **[T / F]** A group of talented teenagers has started their own record label while still in high school.
2. **[T / F]** High school students in Philadelphia started a new music education program to make arts education more practical.
3. **[T / F]** The students are not famous, but they already have a record label and a producer.

[🎧 1-58]

Caleb Autry: I originally wanted to be an engineer, but I realized

15   quickly that it ₃(   ). I knew I had a

    passion for music and I was

    just scared to **pursue** it.

Ruffini: That changed last February,

    when his math and science-

20   focused   High   School,

    George Washington Carver, became the test site for the

    Philadelphia School District's new music production

    program.

test site
実験校

From audio engineering to marketing and distribution, it

25 teaches kids the business ₄( ).

audio engineering
音響工学

Ruffini: Why is it important that this program teaches you not just how to make the record, but the business part of the music industry as well?

distribution
流通・販売

Autry: Young artists going into the music industry today, they're

30 often getting **take**n **advantage of**. That's something that I have a goal of changing, and I feel like kids learning it in school is [*sic*] gonna help with it.

help with it
その役に立つ

Comprehension Check

4.[T / F] Caleb Autry had a passion for engineering, but his teachers told him not to pursue it as a career.

5.[T / F] Caleb's high school became the test site for the Philadelphia School District's new math and science program.

6.[T / F] The new music production program teaches kids everything about the music business, from audio engineering to marketing and distribution.

7.[T / F] Caleb thinks the most important thing about the music program is it teaches students how to make a record.

8.[T / F] Caleb feels the new program will help young artists going into the music business avoid being taken advantage of.

[🎧 1-59]

Ruffini: Caleb grew up playing ₅( ), but he gravitated towards producing.

gravitated towards ~
〜に引きつけられた

35 Is he a good producer or is he a mean producer?

Boy: He definitely challenged me ...

challenged me
僕に刺激を与えて
くれた

Ruffini: I mean, I can take him out of the room, if you need to be honest.

Ruffini: He laid down some loops and

40 **collaborate**d **with** other students on the lyrics and vocals.

laid down some loops
繰り返しの部分を曲
に入れた

Amyronn DesVignes-Pope: They ₆( ) in it and you could hear it on the track.

track
曲

Andy Hurwitz: But ... but heart can only take you so far.

45　*Ruffini:* Which is why professional music producer Andy Hurwitz, who volunteers with the program suggested the students start their own record label. He and Carver High School alum Amyronn DesVignes-Pope, who runs a branding business, help teach the budding moguls how to

50　merchandise their melody.

alum
卒業生

branding business
ブランド戦略

moguls
大物

merchandise
商品を売る

Comprehension Check

9. **[T / F]** Caleb played drums and piano when he was younger, but gradually moved towards producing.
10. **[T / F]** Caleb created some song loops, and worked on the lyrics and vocals of their songs together with other students.
11. **[T / F]** Amyronn DesVignes-Pope said the students did not make enough effort to produce their songs.
12. **[T / F]** Music producer Andy Hurwitz thinks making a big effort is all that is necessary for artists to go far in the music business.
13. **[T / F]** Andy Hurwitz suggested the students start their own record label so they could learn more about the music industry.

[🎧 1-60]

DesVignes-Pope: Everything that we're touching, designing is, top-to-bottom, Carver students to Carver alum, down to the T- shirts and everything.

top-to-bottom
上から下まで徹底
的に

Ruffini: They call the label ... What else? Carver Records.

55　*Hurwitz:* When they played me the music, I was shocked. And so, I $_7$( ) to a couple of people in the industry. I didn't say this is a high school project. I'm working on it ...

Ruffini: You just sent it ...

60　*Hurwitz:* I said, "What do you think of this?"

Ruffini: Yeah.

Hurwitz: And then he's like, "Can we sign them?" I'm like, "Well, they're in high school." He's like, "Oh, we're definitely
65　gonna do this."

I'm like ~
私は~と言った

66

Comprehension Check

14. [T / F] Everything the teens and their advisors produce and design, including branding and merchandising, is done by Carver students or alumni.

15. [T / F] Hurwitz was not surprised by the quality of the songs the teens produced.

16. [T / F] Hurwitz sent a demo of the students' songs to his music industry friends, but they were not interested.

17. [T / F] Hurwitz's music industry friends said they could not sign the students to a record contract because they were still in high school.

[🎵 1-61]

Ruffini: The crew doesn't have a recording **contract** ... yet. But by the end of summer, they plan to release three singles, and an album.

Does this kind of change your trajectory?

70 *Autry:* I feel like it ₈(   ) to the possibilities of the music business.

Ruffini: It also earned Caleb a full scholarship to study the industry at Drexel University this fall. What's the feeling you get

75 when you hear this single finished?

Autry: It's just like, wow. All the hard work we put in this, all came together.

80 *Ruffini:* This may mean the fame ... won't be too far off. For CBS This Morning, Christina Ruffini, Philadelphia.

crew
グループ、一団

trajectory
軌道、通り道

all came together
全てが一つにまとまってよい方向に進んだ

far off
遙か彼方の遠い先のこと

Comprehension Check

18. [T / F] Caleb is no longer scared to pursue his passion for music.

19. [T / F] Caleb feels happy that all their efforts were finally successful.

20. [T / F] The reporter thinks that Caleb and the high school group might be famous someday.

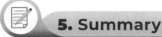 **5. Summary** **1-62**

Fill in the blanks. The first letter of each word is already provided.

Some of the latest ₁(**b**   ) come from Philadelphia, where a group of high school students decided to start their own record ₂(**l**   ). It's part of a new push by the city's school district to make arts education more ₃(**p**   ). The new music production program teaches everything about the music business, from audio engineering to marketing and distribution.   5

The students' group doesn't have ₄(**f**   ) or a name, but they have a budding producer, Caleb Autry. Caleb always knew he had a ₅(**p**   ) for music, but was too scared to ₆(**p**   ) it. He feels the new program will help young artists going into the music business avoid being taken ₇(**a**   ) of. A professional music producer and branding agent are   10 helping the students learn the music industry from top to bottom. The group doesn't have a recording ₈(**c**   ) yet, but they have a new single and a label, Carver Records. Caleb is excited about the possibilities of the music business, and is happy that all their hard work turned out to be successful.

 6. Retelling the News Story **1-63**

Look at the photos below and fill in each blank with the letter of the appropriate answer. Then use the photos and sentences as a guide to retell the news story to your partner or group.

This news story is about young ₁____ who are starting their own record label while still in high school. Their school became a ₂____ site for the city's music production program which teaches the students how to produce and ₃____ music.

Caleb Autry says that young artists should learn about the ₄____ while in school so the music industry will not take ₅____ of them.

Since their music is so good, a professional music producer suggested they start their own ₆____ label. So they are also learning about ₇____, and designing merchandise. They might be ₈____ someday.

a) test   b) business   c) record   d) advantage
e) artists   f) market   g) famous   h) branding

7. In My Opinion

Write a few words about your opinion of this news story. Then share your opinion with your partner or group.

In my opinion, ...
....
....

8. Conversation in Action

CD 1-64

Put the Japanese statements into English. Then listen to check your answers.

Sara: Hey, Jake, I heard you laid down some really cool loops with your band yesterday.

Jake: Yeah, ₁_____
_____. I have so many DMs on *Insta asking me about it I can't *keep up!
（僕たちが心血を注いだすべての仕事が最終的にうまく行ったんだよ）

Sara: Dude, you're like, the *GOAT! Haha.

Jake: Haha. Thanks, but not yet! ₂_____
_____. （僕たちは有名でもないし名前も知られてい
ないけど、僕らみんな音楽に対する情熱を持っているよ）

Sara: It would be great to pursue producing as a career. *Who knows?

You might *land ₃ _____.
（音楽会社とのレコーディング契約か仕事が得られるかもしれないわ）

Jake: Well, maybe. At first, I thought that wouldn't be practical, but it's definitely
*opened my eyes to the possibilities of the music business.

Word Help ***Insta** (short for Instagram): a social media service for sharing photographs and video
    *Example: She shared her new look on her **Insta**.*

    *keep up: to stay level or equal with someone or something   *Example: Technology changes so fast it's hard to **keep up**.*

    *GOAT: "Greatest Of All Time" Someone who is the absolute best at what they do, especially in a sport.   *Example: Shohei Ohtani is the **GOAT**!*

    *Who knows: A rhetorical question asked to express the idea that anything is possible or that anything could happen.   *Example: **Who knows?** Maybe someday you will be rich and famous!*

    *land: to succeed in achieving or getting something   *Example: She **land**ed the starring role in a new film.*

    *opened my eyes: to cause someone to notice or be aware of something important
    *Example: The experience really **opened his eyes** and changed the way he felt about his life.*

Conversation in Action CHALLENGE

Use the vocabulary and phrases you learned in this unit to make a short conversation with your partner. Then practice your conversation with your partner or group.

 9. Critical Thinking

Discuss the following questions with your partner or group. Give reasons to support your opinions.

Understanding the News

1. What new program did the Philadelphia School District start? Why?
2. What can students learn in this program?
3. Why does Caleb Autry think the new program is important?

What Do You Think?

1. Do you think music is important in our lives? Why? / Why not?
2. What kind of music do you enjoy listening to? Why?
3. Prepare a short report about your favorite song, and make a presentation to your group or class. Include information about the artist or band, why you like the song, how it makes you feel, when you like to listen to it, the meaning of the song, etc.

UNIT 9

Vintage Office Gear Making a Comeback During Pandemic

PANDEMIC / LOW-TECH

©CBS MORNINGS

 1. Before You Watch

Look at the title and photos, and then answer the questions.

1. What do the terms, *vintage* and *comeback*, mean?

2. What are these office machines called?
   Have you ever seen or used one before?

2. Word Match

Match each word or phrase with the right definition below.

(   ) **1.** Ken **yearn**ed **for** a chance to get away from his small town and live in a big city.

(   ) **2.** A well-known chef told me how hard it is to pass his skills on to his **apprentice**s.

(   ) **3.** The fishing industry has been **decimate**d by overfishing all over the world.

(   ) **4.** The **landlord** had promised to redecorate the bedrooms before we moved in.

(   ) **5.** Their **vintage** car attracted admiring glances wherever they went.

(   ) **6.** It keeps snowing and I'm getting **sick** and tired **of** shoveling snow from my driveway.

(   ) **7.** Hollywood is full of **aspiring** young actors waiting for their big break into the movies.

(   ) **8.** After years of stress from working for that company, I'm excited to **turn the page** and start in this new position.

---

a. bored with or annoyed about something that has been happening for a long time

b. someone who has agreed to work for a skilled person for a particular period of time in order to learn that person's skills

c. someone who owns a house, apartment, etc., and rents it to other people

d. to want something very much, especially when it is very difficult to get

e. to severely damage something or make something weaker

f. to stop what you are doing and begin something different

g. wanting to have or achieve something (such as a particular career or level of success)

h. something produced in the past, and typical of the period in which it was made

---

3. Getting the Gist (First Viewing)   [Time 02:36]   WEB動画 DVD

Watch the news and choose the right word for each statement.

1. Tom Furrier almost gave up his typewriter business when computers became popular and (released / repaired / replaced) typewriters.

2. Old-style office gear like the typewriter is having a (return / reuse / revival) because many customers want something simple, especially during the pandemic.

4. Getting into Details (Second Viewing)

WEB動画 DVD CD 2-02~06

Watch or listen to the news again. Fill in the blanks and answer the questions.

[CD 2-02]

Anne-Marie Green: The pandemic has changed the way we live. And some people are **yearn**ing **for** life to be ₁(

), which has made a low-tech machine wildly popular. Here's David Wade from our Boston station, WBZ.

5

Comprehension Check

1. [T / F] The changes in our lives caused by the pandemic have made many people yearn for the past, when life was simpler, and technology wasn't so advanced.
2. [T / F] The yearning for a simple life has caused a revival of old-time office wear and other kinds of fashion.

[CD 2-03]

David Wade: At first glance, it is a graveyard: keys and ribbons, space bars and knobs, a mound of machines ...

10

Tom Furrier: Probably four or five hundred.

Wade: ... with stories written and forgotten, years ago.

Furrier: This is all I need.

15 **Wade:** But Tom Furrier has fought to keep the typewriter ₂(   ).

At first glance
一見すると

knobs
セットした紙を手
で回転させるため
のノブ

a mound of ~
大量の

Comprehension Check

3. [T / F] The reporter says Tom Furrier's shop is like a graveyard for long forgotten stories and the old and vintage parts and machines that were used to write them.
4. [T / F] Furrier has less than 400 old and vintage machines in his shop.
5. [T / F] Furrier says he needs several tools to work on old and vintage typewriters.
6. [T / F] Furrier has been trying hard for many years to keep typewriters in existence.

Furrier: At the end of the very first day, this voice in my head said, "This is it."

Wade: That first day at Cambridge Typewriter was 41 years ago.
20 He's gone from young **apprentice** to owner, as the world went from typewriter to tablet.

Furrier: The business was **decimate**d.

Wade: Was there a time where you thought, the ₃(
)?

25 *Furrier:* I was weeks away from telling my **landlord** that that's it, and I'm cashing out and closing down.

Wade: But over the past two decades, typewriters became **vintage**,
30 vintage ₄(   ). And then, the pandemic hit.

Furrier: My phone started ringing off the hook.

**Cambridge
Typewriter**
店舗名

cashing out
資産を売却する

**ringing off the
hook**
電話が鳴りやまない

Comprehension Check

7. **[T / F]** Furrier knew from his first day at work 41 years ago that he did not like working with typewriters.
8. **[T / F]** Furrier started working as an apprentice at the shop and became the owner after many years.
9. **[T / F]** During Furrier's career, office technology advanced, and the world gradually stopped using typewriters.
10. **[T / F]** Furrier told his landlord that he was going to sell all his goods and equipment and close his shop.
11. **[T / F]** During the past 20 years many vintage goods became cool, except for typewriters.
12. **[T / F]** After the pandemic began, many customers telephoned Furrier's shop.

Wade: When the lockdown began,
Tom decided he was gonna
35 start selling his typewriters
curbside so people would
literally window-shop, coming

curbside
歩道で

40 up to the window, pointing at the typewriter they would want to try. And then, Tom says, they would come outside to this bench, to see if that typewriter ... was ₅(
).

Furrier: We are ... the busiest we've ever been in 41 years.

Wade: In a time of doom ... and Zoom, customers tell Tom they want something simple.

doom
破滅

45 *Furrier:* "I'm **sick of** my laptop. I'm throwing it away." "Quick, sell me a typewriter." For real.

For real.
本当だよ、マジで

Abigail Geffken: I almost didn't have any in-person classes. I had more time at home.

Wade: Fifteen-year-old Abigail Geffken is an **aspiring** writer. She
50 ₆( ) during the pandemic.

Geffken: Can I try that one?

Furrier: Sure.

Wade: She's one of Tom's frequent visitors.

Comprehension Check

13. [T / F] During the pandemic lockdown, Furrier started to sell typewriters online.
14. [T / F] Furrier's typewriter shop is busier now than ever before.
15. [T / F] People want a typewriter because they are irritated and tired of using laptops, and want something simple.
16. [T / F] Abigail Geffken spent more time at home because she had almost no in-person classes at her school.
17. [T / F] This is the first time Geffken has visited the typewriter shop.

[🎧2-06]

55 *Geffken:* I think the really cool thing about the ... typewriters is you feel kind of ₇( ) who've used it in the past. And then, of course, there's the clickety-clack everybody loves.

clickety-clack
カタカタという音

Wade: Computers crushed the typewriter ... a pandemic has

60 $_8($). And Tom Furrier is busier than
ever, happily refusing to **turn
the page**.

Furrier: My wife will find me with a
65   spring hook and a screwdriver
in my hand slumped over
a typewriter one day and ...
that'll be it.

spring hook
取り付けや取り外し
をするための先端に
フックが付いている
細長い工具

slumped over ~
〜に前かがみの姿勢
になった状態で

that'll be it
それでおしまいとい
うことになる

Green: That's David Wade from WBZ reporting. CBS Mornings
continues next. I'm Anne-Marie Green.

Comprehension Check

18. [T / F] Geffken says typewriters are cool because you feel a connection to
former users, and they make a unique sound that everyone loves.

19. [T / F] The reporter says the comeback of the typewriter caused by the
pandemic has made him too busy, so he will start working on different
vintage office machines.

20. [T / F] Furrier says he will work on typewriters for as long as he lives.

5. Summary

 2-07

Fill in the blanks. The first letter of each word is already provided.

The COVID-19 pandemic is one of the few things in history that has increased the use of technology in our lives. Many people ₁(**y**   ) for the past when life was simpler. For some, that means a revival of old-time office ₂(**g**   ). Tom Furrier has worked in a typewriter shop for 41 years. He's gone from ₃(**a**   ) to owner, and during that time the world went from typewriter to tablet. Furrier's business was ₄(**d**   ). He nearly told his ₅(**l**   ) that he was cashing out and closing down. But over the past two decades, typewriters became ₆(**v**   ), and vintage became cool. When the pandemic hit, his phone started ringing off the hook and he started selling his typewriters curbside. Furrier said his customers are ₇(**s**   ) of their laptops and want something simple. Abigail Geffken is an ₈(**a**   ) writer. She says typewriters make you feel a connection to former users, and people like the sound they make. Furrier says he will work on typewriters for as long as he lives.

5

10

6. Retelling the News Story

 2-08

Look at the photos below and fill in each blank with the letter of the appropriate answer. Then use the photos and sentences as a guide to retell the news story to your partner or group.

This news story is about a man who owns a typewriter ₁__ business. When computers replaced low-tech machines like typewriters, his business was ₂__. But recently typewriters are becoming popular and cool.

Abigail is a student who likes to write. She often goes to the typewriter shop. She says typewriters make her feel ₃__ to the people who used them. She also loves the ₄__ that typewriters make.

The pandemic has made many people ₅__ of complicated computers and they want something ₆__. Now the typewriter repair shop is ₇__ than ever. Computers replaced typewriters, but a pandemic has brought them back.

a) simpler	b) sick	c) repair	d) sound
e) connected	f) decimated	g) busier	

7. In My Opinion

Write a few words about your opinion of this news story. Then share your opinion with your partner or group.

In my opinion, ...
....
....

8. Conversation in Action

 2-09

Put the Japanese statements into English. Then listen to check your answers.

Jake: Hey, Sara, what's that?

Sara: It's an old typewriter! I found it in the *attic*. My landlord said I could have it. Look! It still works!

Jake: That's awesome. 1_____.
(年代物のオフィス用品がまた流行っているって聞いたけど)

Sara: *It's so fun!* 2_____
_____, before computers and all the high-tech stuff.
(それでもっとシンプルな時代が恋しくなったって私のおばあちゃんが言ってたわ)

Jake: I know, I know. 3_____.
Can I *have a go* at it? (僕はズームや遠隔学習にはもう嫌気がさしてるよ)

Sara: Sure, *go ahead!* I just love the clickety-clack sound.

Jake: Cool. I might get one myself!

 Word Help *attic:** a space or room just below the roof of a building *Example: He kept his old books in the attic.*

*It's so fun:** something enjoyable; slang for: It is *so much* fun. *Example: Going to the beach is so fun.*

*have a go at:** to make an attempt at (doing something) *Example: Can I have a go at your guitar?*

*go ahead:** something that you say to someone to give them permission to do something *Example: "Can I borrow your book?" "Yes, go ahead."*

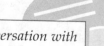

Conversation in Action CHALLENGE

Use the vocabulary and phrases you learned in this unit to make a short conversation with your partner. Then practice your conversation with your partner or group.

9. Critical Thinking

Discuss the following questions with your partner or group. Give reasons to support your opinions.

Understanding the News

1. What old-time office gear has made a comeback during the pandemic? Why?

2. How did Tom Furrier start selling his office gear when the pandemic lockdown began?

3. What does Abigail Geffken like about the machines in Tom Furrier's shop?

What Do You Think?

1. Do you think the COVID-19 pandemic has increased the use of technology in our lives? Why? / Why not? Give some examples.

2. Give some other examples of how the pandemic has affected daily life and lifestyles.

3. Are you interested in vintage goods? If yes, what kind, and why? If not, why not?

UNIT 10

Virtual Tutors
— Teens Offer Free Tutoring to Kids —

EDUCATION / REMOTE LEARNING

1. Before You Watch

Look at the title and photos, and then answer the questions.

1. What is a virtual tutor? What are some other names used for remote learning?

2. Why do you think the teens in the photos are offering free tutoring to kids?

2. Word Match

Match each word or phrase with the right definition below.

(   ) **1.** Rapid climate change has had a **significant** impact on the environment around the world.

(   ) **2.** Successful marketing is all about **connect**ing with your customers, and building good relationships.

(   ) **3.** The campaign is aimed at **reach**ing **out to** young people who are not very interested in the election.

(   ) **4.** She believed she had **come up with** one of the greatest innovations of modern times.

(   ) **5.** The product was never advertised. It became popular by **word of mouth**.

(   ) **6.** Our school festival is just around the corner. I've **sign**ed **on** to help.

(   ) **7.** She **dedicate**d **herself** to the study of chronic diseases in children.

(   ) **8.** I relied on my instincts to **pull** me **through** the crisis.

---

a. to try to get the attention and interest of (someone)

b. to agree to become involved in an organized activity

c. to create a relationship between two or more people, groups, or things

d. information spread by spoken communication

e. very important

f. to give a lot of your time and effort to a particular activity or purpose

g. to think of an idea or plan

h. to survive or endure a difficult or dangerous situation

---

3. Getting the Gist (First Viewing)   [Time 03:49]   WEB動画 DVD

Watch the news and choose the right word for each statement.

1. There is significant (appreciation / concern / surprise) about the increasing inequality gap among children who are learning virtually.

2. The teens came up with the free tutoring idea as a way to (combine / connect / persuade) students and promote social exchange.

Watch or listen to the news again. Fill in the blanks and answer the questions.

[CD 2-11]

Gayle King: Many students have spent this past year going to class
virtually, raising **significant** concerns about a growing
₁( ). But some groups of high

5   school students are finding
ways to bridge that divide,
even as most school districts
reopen safely, by teaching
₂( )
to younger students. Jan

10   Crawford has their stories.

VIRTUAL TUTORS
HIGH SCHOOLERS OFFER FREE TUTORING FOR STUDENTS ACROSS COUNTRY

Ella: Then, suddenly ... Thump! ... Thump! Eek!

Jan Crawford: For most of first and all of second grade, eight-year-old
Ella's classroom ₃( ).

Ella: The sound is coming ...

15   **Emilie:** (inaudible)

Crawford: But behind this screen in her
Virginia home ...

Emilie: This morning we felt so tired.

Crawford: ... is the voice that's kept
20   alive Ella's ₄(
).

Ella: My tutor's name is Miss Emilie. She's kind and really, really
sweet. I love her so much.

Crawford: Miss Emilie is 18-year-old Emilie Kalt, a high school
25   senior in New York City.

Emilie: When my guidance counselor and my school told me about
this opportunity to tutor online, I started tutoring her
in reading. Her reading has improved so much. She's

virtually
ネット上で

**bridge that
divide**
格差を埋める

even as
〜にもかかわらず、
〜なのに

Thump
ドシンという音

Eek
キャーという声

**guidance
counselor**
進路指導の先生

excited to just read everything.

30 *Ella:* Piggy is my best friend.

[🎧 2-12]

Crawford: Ella and Emilie **connect**ed through Intutorly, one of dozens of ₅(   ) programs that was started last spring by high school students.

dozens of ~
数十の～、多数の～

Alex Joel: As high school students, we understand the struggles of
35   virtual learning.

Crawford: Intutorly was created by two Virginia teenagers, Alex and his younger brother Ben.

Ben Joel: We were just dismayed to find that there was an entire
40   generation that would be forced to play catch-up, perhaps ₆(
).

dismayed to ~
～して愕然とする

play catch-up
遅れを取り戻す

Alex: We wanted to do something to help uh ... bridge that gap.

45 *Crawford:* What did you do? How did it start?

Ben: We **reach**ed **out to** our friends, classmates, and family members. And in the early days, we had more tutors than students.

Crawford: How many do you have now?

50 *Ben:* So, we have over 1,000 uh ... students and tutors and about 500 each.

5. [**T** / **F**] Emilie met Ella through Intutorly, a free online tutoring program.
6. [**T** / **F**] Intutorly was created by a dozen school districts.
7. [**T** / **F**] Alex says high school students don't understand how difficult virtual learning is.
8. [**T** / **F**] Alex and Ben Joel were shocked to find that younger students might have to struggle for years to overcome the negative effects of virtual learning.

[🎧2-13]

Girl: And since the Gulf War is a problem now ...

Crawford: Matches like these are happening in other free online tutoring programs also started after the lockdowns by teenagers, like Educove, run by Ian, Subyeta, Joyce, and Christian in New York.

the Gulf War	1991年の湾岸戦争
Matches	縁組み、人と人を結びつけること

55

Ian: We basically **came up with** this idea to connect students as a ₇( ), you know, social exchange, which was something we all were missing um ... with online learning.

social exchange
人と人との社交的なやりとり、関わり合い

60

Subyeta: It was just **word of mouth** and constant, just more contacting. And I think as of now we have around 60 to 70 tutees.

more contacting
ますます連絡が来ています

as of now
今のところ

tutees
家庭教師の教え子

65

Crawford: Their mission also was personal.

Christian: We had a up-close view of this with my two younger brothers. Uh ... They were in sixth and fourth grade at the time. And they were really struggling. Their focus, it sometimes wanes ... with uh ... virtual school. It's harder to keep on track. And it left them a little bit ₈( ) uh ... math and English.

VIRTUAL TUTORS
HIGH SCHOOLERS OFFER FREE TUTORING FOR STUDENTS ACROSS COUNTRY

had a up-close view of ~
～を間近で見た

wanes
徐々に衰える

keep on track
（物事を）順調に進める

70

75

Crawford: Jason is Christian's youngest brother.

Jason: In Christian's school, the teacher would ... walk around the
classroom, and talking to individuals. But then, in online,
80   tea ... teacher would teach the whole class in one sentence
... one session, and no group work.

> **sentence**
> 次のsessionの言い
> 間違え

Comprehension Check

9. [T / F] Ian says he and his friends started Educove because they wanted to
promote online learning.

10. [T / F] Subida says they found teenage tutors for Educove by advertising on
the Internet.

11. [T / F] Christian has personal reasons for starting the tutoring program. His
two younger brothers sometimes lost focus, and it was hard for them to
keep on track with virtual lessons.

12. [T / F] Jason said the teachers in Christian's school teach online, so students
learn in groups.

[🎧 2-14]

Crawford: These teenagers may have first **sign**ed **on** to help others,
but soon realized teaching $_9($).

Christian: Educove ... it was an opportunity for me to find something
85   to really put my mind into [*sic*], and to really **dedicate
myself into** [*sic*]. And it really $_{10}($
) that was sort of left in my heart by not being able to
go to school.

> **put my mind
> into**
> 〜に全力を傾ける

Emilie: It's been hard to deal with the
90   isolation. It's the one thing
that really **pull**ed me **through**
the pandemic.

Hey, I received a heart from
you.

95   Having this bond with Ella, she's not someone I would
have met normally. And ... I really appreciate that.

> **bond**
> 絆、結び付き

Ella: Super sparkly subjects like Glitter Painting ...

Crawford: CBS This Morning, I'm Jan Crawford in Washington.

Ella: History of Sparkle Grove Forest.

13. [T / F] The experience of teaching others helped the teens learn how to put their minds to something, and cope with isolation.

14. [T / F] Tutoring Ella online during the pandemic made Emilie feel frustrated and isolated.

15. [T / F] Emilie feels sad that she couldn't bond with Ella because she couldn't meet her in person.

5. Summary

 2-15

Fill in the blanks. The first letter of each word is already provided.

There is $_1$(s   ) concern about the growing inequality gap among children who are learning virtually. But some high school students are bridging that $_2$(d   ) by teaching what they've learned to younger students. Eight-year-old Ella has been learning online for almost two years. Her reading tutor is Emilie, a high school senior from New York. Ella and Emilie connected through Intutorly, one of dozens of free online $_3$(t   ) programs started by high school students. Alex and Ben Joel say high school students understand the $_4$(s   ) of virtual learning and were worried that an entire generation might fall too far behind in their studies. So, they $_5$(r   ) out to their friends and others to start Intutorly. Other groups of teens $_6$(c   ) up with similar programs, and the idea spread by word of mouth. The teens say these programs promote social exchange and keep students on $_7$(t   ). And $_8$(s   ) on to help others helped them learn how to dedicate themselves to something, and cope with isolation.

5

10

15

6. Retelling the News Story

 CD 2-16

Look at the photos below and fill in each blank with the letter of the appropriate answer. Then use the photos and sentences as a guide to retell the news story to your partner or group.

This is a news story about a gap among children who are learning ₁__. Many are ₂__. High school students are helping to make online learning more ₃__ by teaching younger students.

Eight-year-old Ella's reading tutor is a high school senior named Emilie. Ella and Emilie met through one of the many free online ₄__ programs started by teenage students. Emilie says Ella's reading has ₅__ very much.

High school students say they understand the ₆__ of virtual learning. The ₇__ of teaching others helped the teens learn how to put their minds to something, and cope with ₈__.

a) isolation	b) struggles	c) falling behind	d) improved
e) tutoring	f) equal	g) experience	h) virtually

7. In My Opinion

Write a few words about your opinion of this news story. Then share your opinion with your partner or group.

In my opinion, ...
....
....

8. Conversation in Action 2-17

Put the Japanese statements into English. Then listen to check your answers.

Sara: Hey, Jake, what's up?

Jake: Hey, Sara. **Just a sec.* 1_____.

    （もうすぐオンラインの個人教授の時間が終わるから）

  OK ... **I'm done.*

Sara: I didn't know you were tutoring. **How's it going?*

Jake: I really like it. 2_____

_____,

so I reached out and signed on to help out. （遠隔授業を受けている学生の中には授業について行くのに苦労している人たちがいるからね）

Sara: Great. Who came up with the idea?

Jake: The Student Resource Center. But it's not on their website yet. 3_____

_____. （それについては口コミで聞いたんだよ）

Sara: I'm sure it will be a **big help* and keep students on track.

Word Help

*Just a sec(ond): just a minute/moment/second: used to ask someone to wait for a short period of time
 *Example: **Just a sec!** I'll open the door as soon as I find my key.*

*I'm done: to finish, or complete a task
 *Example: "Did you finish your report?" "Yes, **I'm done**."*

*How's it going? / How is it going?: used to ask how a situation or activity is progressing
 *Example: "I heard you got a new job. **How's it going?**" "It's going well, thanks." / "It's a little hard, but I like it a lot."*

*big help: to be extremely useful, or make it easier to do something
 *Example: Thanks for the ride to the airport. You've been a **big help**!*

 Conversation in Action CHALLENGE

Use the vocabulary and phrases you learned in this unit to make a short conversation with your partner. Then practice your conversation with your partner or group.

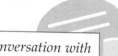

9. Critical Thinking

Discuss the following questions with your partner or group. Give reasons to support your opinions.

Understanding the News

1. What motivated Alex and Ben to create Intutorly?
2. How did Ian and his classmates come up with the idea for Educove? What personal reason did Christian have for participating in the tutoring program?
3. What lessons did the teenagers learn from teaching others?

What Do You Think?

1. Why might virtual learning be difficult for some students?
2. What are the advantages and disadvantages of online and virtual learning classes?
3. Do you prefer in-person, remote, or hybrid (blended) learning classes? Why?

UNIT 11

Thanksgiving
— A Time of Gratitude and Reflection —

HOLIDAY / THANKSGIVING

1. Before You Watch

Look at the title and photos, and then answer the questions.

1. What does the word, *thanksgiving* mean to you?

2. What do you know about the American Holiday of Thanksgiving?

2. Word Match

Match each word or phrase with the right definition below.

(   ) **1.** Let's **celebrate** your birthday together this year.

(   ) **2.** You can apply for a visa by mail, but it's quicker if you go to the embassy **in person**.

(   ) **3.** It's important to take what we learn from an experience and use it to **better ourselves**.

(   ) **4.** I'm very **thankful** to spend this Thanksgiving with you all.

(   ) **5.** I would love for you to come over. I need the **company**.

(   ) **6.** They opened a **shelter** to provide temporary housing for the city's homeless.

(   ) **7.** Our teacher **insist**s that we be on time for class.

(   ) **8.** Allowing pets in the workplace can produce a number of **tangible** benefits.

---

a. happy or grateful about something that has happened

b. to do things that will improve oneself, or make one a more successful person

c. a place to live or that gives protection from bad weather or danger

d. to acknowledge (a significant or happy day or event) with a social gathering or enjoyable activity

e. easily seen or recognized, able to be touched or felt

f. being with another or others, especially in a way that provides friendship and enjoyment

g. to demand that something happen or that somebody agree to do something

h. being actually present, or going somewhere to do something yourself rather than doing it online, by phone, video chat, etc.

---

3. Getting the Gist (First Viewing)   [Time 03:13]

WEB動画   DVD

Watch the news and choose the right word for each statement.

1. Thanksgiving is a time to celebrate, and to remember the less (fortunate / friendly / lively), and think about self-improvement and helping others.

2. In (contrast / difference / opposite) to 2020, many Americans will be able to gather together to celebrate a traditional Thanksgiving in person.

Watch or listen to the news again. Fill in the blanks and answer the questions.

[2-19]

Gayle King: This week in two days, families will gather to **celebrate** Thanksgiving. In contrast to last year, many of us will get to do that **in person**. The holiday, as you know, is a time to celebrate. But as Sunday Morning correspondent Lee

5   Cowan reminds us, it's also
a time to remember ₁(

),
and think about ways to
better ourselves, and others.

get to ~
〜できるようになる

10 **Man:** Can you say, "Gobble, gobble"?

Woman and boy: Gobble, gobble.

Gobble
ガツガツ食べる

Lee Cowan: Remember last Thanksgiving? Most of us were just **thankful** 2020 was almost over. This year, ₂(
). Our Thanksgiving traditions
15   have ... mostly returned.

Girl: Pie.

Woman: What do you think?

Girl: Pie.

Comprehension Check

1. **[T / F]** Gayle King says families will gather to celebrate Thanksgiving for two days.
2. **[T / F]** Thanksgiving is a traditional time of celebration, but it's also a time for self-improvement, and remembering and helping others who are less fortunate than ourselves.
3. **[T / F]** Compared to 2020, Lee Cowan says the usual Thanksgiving Day traditions have not returned, and people will still have virtual Thanksgiving dinners.

[2-20]

Cowan: But, as we bow our heads, in the **company** of all of those we
20   care most about, not very far away ... are plenty, suffering

bow our heads
食前に頭を垂れて
神に祈る

without ... those with no
shelter, who are hungry or
struggling with addiction,
or mental health. Sometimes

25 both. For them, Thanksgiving
Day ... is ₃(

). Their friends — and family?
Maybe they have none. The unluckiest among them are
dreadfully alone, the feeling truly magnified, imagining

30 the rest of us ... gathering together.

without
（あるべきものが）
ない、欠けた状態で

dreadfully
恐ろしいくらい

magnified
大きなものとなる

Comprehension Check

4. [T / F] Cowan says that while people are enjoying Thanksgiving dinner with their loved ones, there are many people nearby who are hungry, homeless, and suffering.

5. [T / F] Thanksgiving Day is just an ordinary day for those who have no place to live, and are struggling with addiction or mental illness.

6. [T / F] Imagining others gathering together with friends and family on Thanksgiving Day makes the less fortunate feel like they are not alone.

[🎧2-21]

Cowan: But the ₄(   ) that we hear so much
about isn't some ghostly apparition. At this time of year,
its touch ... can be every bit as real as a handshake. After
all, no one is forcing us to gather spare change at the

35 traffic light, give to the man or
woman with a cardboard sign.
Nobody **insist**s we rummage
through our closets to find
warm clothes to give to those

40 whom we've never met.

ghostly
apparition
幽霊、亡霊の出現

every bit
全く

spare change
余った小銭

rummage
through ~
~をかき回して捜す

Woman at a food shelter: Thank you. You guys have a blessed
Thanksgiving.

Cowan: Our schedules, usually ₅(   ) the rest
of the year, mysteriously open up. And maybe ... we even

45 step foot in a house of worship, for the first time in a long,
long while.

blessed
楽しい、喜びにあ
ふれた

step foot in a
house of worship
信仰の館に足を踏み
入れる

for the first time
in a long, long
while
本当にひさしぶりに

7. [T / F] The spirit of the Thanksgiving holiday can be seen, and looks like the image of a ghost.

8. [T / F] The touch of the spirit of Thanksgiving can be felt when we do something kind, like give our spare change or used clothing to strangers in need.

9. [T / F] People are usually too busy to volunteer during the Thanksgiving holiday season.

10. [T / F] The reporter says that people who seldom go to a house of worship might go there at Thanksgiving time.

[🎧2-22]

Woman: Oh, be careful. Yum, yum, yum.

Cowan: Whatever you believe the holiday spirit to be, it does seem
to be **tangible**. It brings those
50 who are not at our table into
gentle focus. It reminds us
how lucky we are. And it
makes all the disparate parts
of our country seem, even for
55 a few weeks, like we're gathered around some common
hearth. Of course, keeping that spirit all year long isn't
easy. Maybe that's why every 12 months, we get a $_6($
).

Girls: And we hope you have a very good Thanksgiving. Happy
60 Thanksgiving! Happy Thanksgiving!

Yum, yum, yum.
おいしい、おいしい

**bring ~ into
gentle focus**
~にやさしく焦点を
当てる

disparate
全く異なるものから
構成されている

hearth
暖炉前

11. [T / F] The Thanksgiving holiday spirit focuses our awareness and concern on the welfare of people that we don't know or notice during the rest of the year.

12. [T / F] The Thanksgiving holiday reminds us of how unfortunate we are compared to others.

13. [T / F] No matter how different and diverse America is, the spirit of the Thanksgiving season seems to bring Americans together, even if it's just for a short time.

14. [T / F] Keeping the spirit of good will and unity of the Thanksgiving holiday throughout the year is difficult.

5. Summary

 2-23

Fill in the blanks. The first letter of each word is already provided.

Thanksgiving is a traditional time to 1(c   ) and be 2(t   ) for what we have. It is also a time to remember the less fortunate, and think about ways to 3(b   ) ourselves, and others. Holiday get-togethers and family gatherings were limited in 2020 because of COVID-19. But in contrast to last year, the usual Thanksgiving Day traditions have mostly returned, and people will be able to have Thanksgiving dinner in 4(p   ). However, while we are celebrating and enjoying the company of our loved ones, there are people nearby with no 5(s   ) and who are alone, hungry, and are struggling with addiction or mental illness. The spirit of Thanksgiving is 6(t   ). And though no one insists, we try to do something kind for others, like give our spare change or used clothing to strangers in need. We find time in our busy schedules to volunteer or attend religious services. Thanksgiving 7(r   ) us of how lucky we are, and also to think about others. No matter how disparate America is, the spirit of the Thanksgiving season seems to 8(b   ) Americans together, even if it's just for a short time.

5

10

15

6. Retelling the News Story

 2-24

Look at the photos below and fill in each blank with the letter of the appropriate answer. Then use the photos and sentences as a guide to retell the news story to your partner or group.

This news story is about Thanksgiving Day in America. Families and friends get together to 1___ and have a 2___ turkey dinner. Last year, some people had to meet virtually because of the pandemic. But this year, many will meet in 3___.

It's a time for people to be 4___ for what they have. It's also a time to think about, and be 5___ to others, especially those who are in 6___.

Thanksgiving seems to bring all Americans together, even for a short time. Keeping that 7___ spirit all year long isn't easy. But every year is another 8___ to try again.

| a) holiday | b) person | c) thankful | d) celebrate |
| e) kind | f) chance | g) need | h) traditional |

7. In My Opinion

Write a few words about your opinion of this news story. Then share your opinion with your partner or group.

In my opinion, ...
....
....

8. Conversation in Action

 2-25

Put the Japanese statements into English. Then listen to check your answers.

Jake: Sara, *do you have any plans* for Thanksgiving?

Sara: I do. We're going to my Grandma's house for Thanksgiving Dinner. How about you?

Jake: We're having ours at home. And some relatives are *coming all the way from* New York.

Sara: Awesome! No more virtual dinners like last year! 1_____
_____. （感謝祭の伝統がほぼ戻ってきてみんな興奮しているわ）

Jake: Uh huh. Me, too. 2_____.
（僕たちはまだ気をつけなければいけないけど、感謝祭をまた直接会ってお祝いするのはいいね）

Sara: Yeah. *I know what you mean.* It's been a tough year for everyone, but 3 there's _____. （いつも何か感謝をすべきことがあるわ）

Jake: That's for sure! Well, it's getting late. *I've gotta go.* Happy Thanksgiving!

Sara: Happy Thanksgiving!

Word Help ***do you have any plans:** informal for, Do you have anything in mind that you would like to do
Example: ***Do you have any plans*** *for the weekend?*

*coming all the way from: to travel a long distance   *Example: My aunt is **coming all the way***
from *Kyushu to attend the wedding.*

* I know what you mean: used to suggest that the listener agrees with, and understands what
has been said   *Example: "That movie is hard to understand." "**I know what you mean.**"*

* I've gotta go/I gotta go: informal for I have got to go, or I have to go; used to say you must
leave   *Example:* ***I've gotta go,*** *or I'll miss my train!*

 ## Conversation in Action CHALLENGE

Use the vocabulary and phrases you learned in this unit to make a short conversation with
your partner. Then practice your conversation with your partner or group.

 ## 9. Critical Thinking

Discuss the following questions with your partner or group. Give reasons to support
your opinions.

Understanding the News

1. How does Gayle King describe the Thanksgiving holiday? How will the
   celebration of Thanksgiving be different from last year?

2. Why does Lee Cowan say Thanksgiving Day is just another day for some
   people?

3. What are some examples of how people show kindness to others during
   the Thanksgiving holiday season, or do things they don't usually do?

4. What examples does Cowan give to show that the spirit of Thanksgiving is
   tangible?

What Do You Think?

1. Why and how do Americans celebrate Thanksgiving?

2. What other countries have a thanksgiving holiday? Why and how do they
   celebrate it?

3. Thanksgiving is a time of *gratitude* and *reflection*. What do these terms
   mean, and why are they so important, especially during this holiday?

4. Make a list of five things that you are grateful for, and why.

UNIT 12

You've Got a Friend
— New York Woman Starts Movement to Unite Strangers —

CONNECTION / SOCIAL MEDIA

TikTok
VIEWED MORE THAN **14 MILLION TIMES**

A MORE PERFECT UNION
YOU'VE GOT A FRIEND
NYC WOMAN CREATES MOVEMENT FOR STRANGERS TO MEET UP AND CONNECT

JUNE 5TH
2PM - CEDAR HILL
CENTRAL PARK

FOLLOW ON INSTA!
@MarissaMeizz
@NoMoreLonelyFriends

1. Before You Watch

Look at the title and photos, and then answer the questions.

1. How do you feel when you cannot meet your friends?

2. Why do you think the woman in the photo wants to unite strangers?

98

2. Word Match

Match each word or phrase with the right definition below.

(   ) **1.** If we don't invite him, he will feel **exclude**d.

(   ) **2.** When she woke up and checked her phone, she found that her tweet had gone **viral**.

(   ) **3.** We've **identifi**ed some strategic areas where we can concentrate our efforts.

(   ) **4.** That investment **end**ed **up** cost**ing** me a lot of money.

(   ) **5.** I'm planning to **hang out** with my friends, watch a lot of TV, and eat lots of junk food this weekend.

(   ) **6.** I invited him for eight o'clock, but he didn't **show up** until nine-thirty.

(   ) **7.** Living in a foreign country is interesting, but you might **feel isolated** sometimes.

(   ) **8.** You can't change what has already happened, so don't waste your time thinking about it. **Move on**, let go, and get over it.

---

a. to spend time relaxing in a particular place, or socializing with someone or a group of people

b. to not allow someone to take part in something, especially in a way that seems wrong or unfair

c. to finally arrive, especially by a roundabout or lengthy route or process

d. to recognize or be able to prove who or what someone or something is

e. to accept a situation that cannot be changed, and be ready to deal with new experiences

f. to spread quickly and widely among internet users via social networking sites, email, etc.

g. to be or feel separated from others

h. to arrive for a gathering or event

---

3. Getting the Gist (First Viewing) [Time 03:06]

Watch the news and choose the right word for each statement.

1. Drew Harden (listened / overheard / oversaw) two strangers planning to exclude a friend named Marissa from their party.

2. Marissa started a movement where strangers meet up safely outdoors at Central Park once a month for a picnic. It creates a safe space for new friendships to (express / form / meet).

Watch or listen to the news again. Fill in the blanks and answer the questions.

[2-27]

Vladimir Duthiers: Researchers say the pandemic has deepened
America's epidemic of
loneliness. Among young
adults ages 18 to 25, a
5 staggering 61 percent
reported serious loneliness
during the pandemic. Now,
as our Jamie Wax shows us, one New York woman is on
a mission to ₁(   ) each other at
10 indoor [*sic*] gatherings.

Drew Harden: If your name is Marissa, please listen up.

Jamie Wax: It all began with a rather unkind video. While out for a
walk, Drew Harden overheard two strangers planning
a party, part of their plan to **exclude** a friend named
15 Marissa.

Harden: They are choosing to do it the weekend you're away ...

Wax: It's quite frankly everyone's worst nightmare.

Harden: Your friends doing, you know, mental gymnastics to
₂(   ) to a birthday party.

epidemic 蔓延・流行	
staggering 驚くほど膨大な	
on a mission to ~ ～しようと懸命になっている	
indoor outdoorの間違い	
worst nightmare 最悪の夢	
mental gymnastics 頭の体操	

Comprehension Check

1. [T / F] The pandemic has caused loneliness in America to increase, especially among young people.
2. [T / F] A New York woman is trying to help strangers gather together and meet.
3. [T / F] Drew Harden was at a party when he overheard two people planning to exclude their friend, Marissa from a birthday party.
4. [T / F] The two people planning the birthday party decided to schedule it on a weekday when Marissa was out of town.
5. [T / F] The reporter says being excluded from a party by friends would be a very unpleasant experience for anyone.
6. [T / F] Harden thinks the way the two friends were planning to exclude Marissa was unreasonable and unkind.

[🎧 2-28]

20 *Wax:* The 23-year-old recorded what he heard, posted it to TikTok, and ₃(   ) this Marissa.

Harden: TikTok, help me find Marissa.

Wax: The post **went viral**, viewed more than 14 million times. Within
25 a day, 23-year-old Marissa Meizz was **identifi**ed.

Marissa Meizz: That **end**ed **up** gett**ing** back to me and uh ... I was ... I mean ... just ... sad. It was sad. I got one text message basically confirming that it was them, and that was it.

30 *Wax:* Marissa pushed through the sadness and pain, turning her unexpected ₄(   ) into a mission of inclusivity.

Marissa: A bunch of people were messaging me, "I would love
35 to be your friend. Let's meet up, let's **hang out**. I am lonely. I'm sad," whatever. And I took that and I was like, why not ... have everyone meet up in one place to meet each other?

posted	投稿した

confirming ~
〜であると認めた

and that was it
（謝罪などがなくて）それだけだった

pushed through ~
〜を押し除けて進んだ

inclusivity
誰も排除しないこと

A bunch of ~
たくさんの

I was like ~
〜と私は言った
（＝I said）

Comprehension Check

7. [T / F] Harden recorded what he overheard and posted it to TikTok, and asked users to find Marissa.

8. [T / F] Harden's TikTok post did not receive many views, so it took a long time to find Marissa.

9. [T / F] Marissa was sad because she didn't know the people Harden talked about in his TikTok post.

10. [T / F] Marissa overcame her sadness, and decided to use her social media fame to connect with others who felt excluded.

11. [T / F] Marissa received several messages from people who were also lonely or sad and wanted to meet up and hang out together.

12. [T / F] After receiving so many messages, Marissa came up with the idea to have everyone meet up in one place so they could all meet each other.

40　*Marissa:* We are having our first, friend, picnic meetup.

　　Wax: Born was "No More Lonely Friends," a movement where strangers meet up safely outdoors at Central Park once a month for a picnic. It creates a safe space for ₅(

).

45　*Marissa:* I never expected more than, I don't know, 20, 30 people and when like, 200 people **show**ed **up**, just … blows my mind.

　　Wax: The popularity of "No More Lonely Friends" has moved beyond the Big Apple, with Marissa hosting picnics in
50　　other cities like Boston and LA.

　　Wax: Is this a story about something beautiful that came from all of us **feel**ing **isolated** during the pandemic?

　　Marissa: I think uh … it was a really cool thing to see so many people ₆(   ) their mental health
55　during the pandemic. And there were parts that, we were so isolated … and so, coming together with everyone, being like this together is just so …
60　just so amazing.

picnic meetup	野外で行う会合・オフ会
blows my mind	圧倒された、驚いた
coming together with ~	~と集まる、一緒になる

Comprehension Check

13. [T / F] "No More Lonely Friends" is a movement where old friends meet up at Central Park once a month for a picnic.
14. [T / F] The movement creates a safe space for new friendships to form because strangers meet in a group, and it's safer to meet outdoors during the pandemic.
15. [T / F] Marissa was expecting more than 200 people to show up for the first friend meetup.
16. [T / F] "No More Lonely Friends" is not popular outside New York, so Marissa is not hosting meetup picnics in other cities.
17. [T / F] Marissa thinks it's amazing that so many people were honest about sharing their feelings of loneliness and isolation during the pandemic.

[🎧2-30]

Wax: Strangers she can now call friends, including Drew, who
started it all with his TikTok post.

Harden: I was so ... inspired by her response to be like, "You know
what, I'm good. I'm moving on." I think it's a [*sic*] really
65   powerful just to speak to ₇(   ),
and how starved of it we've been during the pandemic.

Wax: Marissa hopes to continue connecting lonely strangers
together, and has a goal to host picnics in all 50 states.

Marissa: It's a free event that everyone is
70   welcome, ₈(
), and ... just I just would
love for more people to know
so that they can make friends
too, and just feel welcome as
75   everybody else does.

Wax: No more lonely friends.

Marissa: No more lonely friends.

Wax: For CBS This Morning, Jamie Wax, New York.

| inspired |
| 刺激を受けた |
| **I'm good.** |
| 私はだいじょうぶ |
| **starved of ~** |
| ～に飢えている、～ |
| が不足している |

feel welcome
歓迎されていると
感じる

Comprehension Check

18. [T / F] Drew Harden was disappointed in Marissa's response to being excluded
from the birthday party by her friends.

19. [T / F] Harden thinks friendships, and people's ability to make friends have not
been affected by the pandemic.

---

 5. Summary   2-31

Fill in the blanks. The first letter of each word is already provided.

Researchers say the pandemic has deepened America's ₁(e   ) of
loneliness, especially among young people. A man overheard two strangers
planning to ₂(e   ) a friend named Marissa from their birthday
party. He recorded what he heard and posted it to TikTok, and asked users

103

to find Marissa. The post went ₃(**v**   ), and Marissa Meizz was
₄(**i**   ). That post ₅(**e**   ) up getting back to Marissa,
and made her feel sad. But she moved on, and used her social media fame to
connect with others who felt excluded. Marissa received many messages from
people who wanted to meet up and ₆(**h**   ) out together. She came
up with an idea for "No More Lonely Friends," a way to have everyone meet up
safely outdoors at Central Park once a month for a picnic, and to make friends.
More than 200 people ₇(**s**   ) up. It became popular, and Marissa
is hosting picnics across America. Marissa thinks it's cool that so many people
were open about sharing their feelings of loneliness and ₈(**i**   )
during the pandemic.

6. Retelling the News Story

CD 2-32

Look at the photos below and fill in each blank with the letter of the appropriate answer.
Then use the photos and sentences as a guide to retell the news story to your partner or
group.

This news story is about a New York woman named Marissa,
who is on a mission to help ₁___ meet each other in outdoor
gatherings. A man overheard two people planning to
₂___ their friend, Marissa from a birthday party. He posted
what he heard to TikTok and asked users to find Marissa.

The post went ₃___ and Marissa was soon ₄___. She felt sad and
hurt, but she ₅___ her sadness and pain. She got a bunch of
messages asking her to ₆___. Marissa came up with an idea
to have everyone meet up in one place so they could all meet
each other.

More than 200 people ₇___. Marissa was surprised to find a lot
of people who have been feeling ₈___ and sad, especially during
the pandemic. Her "No More Lonely Friends" movement was
born, and has spread to other cities in America.

a) isolated	b) exclude	c) showed up	d) lonely strangers
e) identified	f) hang out	g) pushed through	h) viral

7. In My Opinion

Write a few words about your opinion of this news story. Then share your opinion with your partner or group.

In my opinion, ...

....

....

8. Conversation in Action

 2-33

Put the Japanese statements into English. Then listen to check your answers.

Sara: Hey, Jake, What's up? You look a little down.

Jake: **I'm good*, I guess. But honestly, sometimes all the isolation caused by the pandemic **gets to me*, you know?

Sara: **I hear you*. It's like an epidemic of loneliness. It's ₁_____

_____. （以前のように一緒に過ごすことができないのはつらいわね）

Jake: I thought using chat apps would keep me more in touch. But

₂_____.

（でも本当に話す機会が少なくなって、結局会話はメールに頼っちゃってるな）

Sara: Yeah. ₃_____

_____. （ソーシャルメディアは人々とのつながりを保

つのに役だってるけど、実際に会って付き合うのがずっといいわね）

> **Word Help** ***I'm good:** used to express that one is not too hurt or sick to do something
> *Example: "Are you feeling OK? You look a little sick" **"I'm good. I just need to rest a little."***
>
> ***gets to me:** to make someone feel annoyed or upset
> *Example: I'm under a lot of pressure at work, and sometimes it **gets to me**.*
>
> ***I hear you:** used to show you heard, and also understood and agree with what someone
> said *Example: "This coffee shop is so expensive!" **"I hear you**. Let's go to a cheaper one."*

Conversation in Action CHALLENGE

Use the vocabulary and phrases you learned in this unit to make a short conversation with your partner. Then practice your conversation with your partner or group.

9. Critical Thinking

Discuss the following questions with your partner or group. Give reasons to support your opinions.

Understanding the News

1. Why did Drew Harden want to contact Marissa?
2. How did he find her?
3. What movement did Marissa create? Why?

What Do You Think?

1. What are three qualities of a good friend?
2. Would you attend an event like "No More Lonely Friends" to meet and make friends? Why? / Why not?
3. What is the difference between being alone and being lonely?
   Have you ever felt lonely during the pandemic? Why? / Why not?
4. Do you think social media isolates people, or brings them together? Why?

UNIT 13

Japan's Love of Vending Machines

JAPAN / CONSUMERISM

 1. Before You Watch

Look at the title and photos, and then answer the questions.

1. What kinds of products can you buy from vending machines in Japan?

2. How often do you use vending machines? What do you usually buy?

2. Word Match

Match each word or phrase with the right definition below.

(   ) **1.** Your **infatuation with** him is clouding your judgment.

(   ) **2.** A *maneki-neko* is a ceramic figurine of a cat with a paw raised in a **beckon**ing gesture. It is often displayed at the entrance of Japanese shops.

(   ) **3.** She skipped normal meals to satisfy her **craving for** chocolate and crisps.

(   ) **4.** My brother likes **junk food** such as hot dogs and fizzy drinks.

(   ) **5.** Sugar-**free** sweets are available and are a healthier option for people with diabetes.

(   ) **6.** This coffee is **nasty**! Don't drink it.

(   ) **7.** I'm quite an **introvert** and seldom go to parties or enjoy situations that are out of my comfort zone.

(   ) **8.** A passer-by **capture**d the whole incident on her smartphone.

---

a. someone who is shy, quiet, and prefers to spend time alone rather than often being with other people

b. a strong feeling of attraction, fascination, or obsession towards someone or something, often for a short period of time

c. used at the end of words to mean "without"

d. to record or take a picture of something using a camera

e. food that is quick and easy to prepare and eat, but is unhealthy, because it is high in fat, sugar, or artificial substances

f. a powerful desire for something

g. to signal (someone) with your hand to tell that person to come closer; to attract

h. bad or very unpleasant; especially to the senses

---

 3. Getting the Gist (First Viewing)   [Time 03:19]   WEB動画 DVD

Watch the news and choose the right word for each statement.

1. Compared to other countries, Japan is the world (administrator / director / leader) in the variety and number of vending machines.

2. A low crime rate and a (desire / necessity / requirement) for convenience have made Japan a mecca for vending machines.

4. Getting into Details (Second Viewing)

WEB動画 DVD CD 2-35~38

Watch or listen to the news again. Fill in the blanks and answer the questions.

[CD 2-35]

Ad: When Betty returns, she gives the operator the number on her
receipt and deposits the proper amount in the coin slot.
The operator again opens the locker by remote control.
And there's the garment: cleaned and pressed.

5 *Dana Jacobson:* America's love affair with vending machines goes
back generations even before that 1940s advertisement.
Today, there are about $_1$(   ) vending
machines in the United States serving us sodas, snacks,
and sundries, to the tune of nearly $22 billion a year, or

10 quick math, $62 a person. But for sheer mind-numbing
variety and volume, Japan
is hands down the vending
machine $_2$(

). Lucy Craft dug out
15 some spare change for this
story.

deposits お金を入れて支払う	
garment: cleaned and pressed 衣服が洗浄されアイロンがかけられた状態で（出てきます）	
sundries 雑貨	
to the tune of ~ ～の額まで	
quick math 単純計算で	
sheer mind-numbing 完全に心を萎えさせるような	
hands down 間違いなく	
spare change 余った小銭	

Comprehension Check

1. [T / F] America's enthusiasm for vending machines began after the 1940s.
2. [T / F] Not many Americans use vending machines today.
3. [T / F] Japan has the largest variety and number of vending machines in the world.

[CD 2-36]

Lucy Craft: It's hard to overstate Japan's total **infatuation with** the
vending machine. The country has so many there's one
for every 30 people. The blinking lights and friendly

20 glow seem to **beckon** from every nook and cranny. Banks
of vending machines line busy walkways. Super slim
versions sprout from lonely corners, making it nearly
impossible to escape the pause that refreshes.

A low crime rate and a **craving for** convenience have
25 made Japan a mecca for automated self-service. **Junk**

glow 柔らかな光	
from every nook and cranny 至る所から	
Banks of ~ line busy walkways ～が混み合った歩道に列をなして並んでいる	
sprout 急に出現する	
pause that refreshes コカコーラの有名な宣伝用フレーズ	

food is actually ₃( ) than options like fresh bananas, or artisanal soup broth. That's a whole grilled fish right inside the bottle.

Comprehension Check
---

4. [T / F] Japan's vending machines are too wide to fit into walkways and other small spaces.

5. [T / F] You can easily find a vending machine nearby when you want to take a break and have something to drink or eat.

6. [T / F] A safe environment and strong preference for convenience make Japan an ideal place for vending machines.

7. [T / F] You are more likely to find a vending machine selling junk food than healthy food like fresh fruit and fish broth.

[CD 2-37]

Craft: So, you've got the munchies.
30 If you're in Japan, you're in luck. There's a wide variety of treats to choose from, like rhino beetles, scorpions, grasshoppers, and giant water
35 bugs — all full of protein and gluten-**free**.

So, I went for the chocolate covered super worms. That's **nasty**.

At Tokyo's Haneda Airport, the ₄( ) also
40 buys a tea-serving sprite. A coffee machine that produces latte foam art. Planner, Masashi Sakurai said, "There are a lot of opinions about this, but Japanese are basically shy. Vending machines are perfect for **introvert**s."

There's a tyranny of choice ... from plush toys, to wood
45 crafting kits, to collectibles like trading cards, popstar posters, and cat sushi trinkets.

---

artisanal soup broth
職人が作った出汁

grilled fish
焼き魚

you've got the munchies
無性におなかがすいたとします

rhino beetles, scorpions, grasshoppers, and giant water bugs
カブトムシやサソリ、バッタや大きな水生昆虫

protein タンパク質

tea-serving sprite
お茶を運ぶ妖精

a tyranny of ~
たくさんの～

plush toys
ハイカラなおもちゃ

wood crafting kits
木製の工作キット

collectibles
収集価値のある物

trinkets ちょっとしたアクセサリー

Comprehension Check

8. **[T / F]** The reporter says vending machines in Japan sell a large variety of snacks, including unusual items like insects and worms.

9. **[T / F]** Although eating insects might seem nasty to some people, they are actually healthy, because they contain protein and are gluten-free.

10. **[T / F]** Masashi Sakurai says vending machines are not popular in Japan because the Japanese are introverts and are too shy to use them.

11. **[T / F]** The reporter says vending machines offer a limited number of choices for consumers.

[🎧2-38]

Craft: At this Buddhist temple, good-luck amulets sold as discreetly as sodas. Even higher-end products get the vending machine treatment, like Tiffany perfume and freshwater
50 pearls.

Vending machines are now ₅(   ).
This image by photographer Eiji Ohashi auctioned in London for more than
55 $40,000. "Shining there in the snow, the vending machine seemed human to me," he said.

Ohashi has amassed 1,000 more photos. After 13 years
60 spent **captur**ing the vending machine in the wild, he said he's only begun to ₆(   ).

For CBS This Morning Saturday, Lucy Craft, Tokyo.

good-luck amulets お守り

discreetly 控えめに

higher-end より高級な

freshwater pearls 淡水真珠

auctioned 競売で売られた

has amassed 蓄積している

in the wild 荒野の中で

Comprehension Check

12. **[T / F]** The reporter says you can buy both ordinary items like sodas, and special ones like amulets, from the vending machines at a Buddhist temple.

13. **[T / F]** Expensive and high-quality products are not sold in vending machines in Japan.

14. **[T / F]** Photos of vending machines have become fine art, like painting and sculpture, and are very expensive.

15. **[T / F]** Eiji Ohashi has spent 13 years taking more than 1,000 pictures of vending machines in various places all over Japan, but feels he has only just begun to photograph them.

5. Summary

Fill in the blanks. The first letter of each word is already provided.

America's love affair with vending machines goes back generations. But for sheer number and variety, Japan is hands down the vending machine capital of the world. It's hard to overstate Japan's total $_1$(**i**   ) with the vending machine. The blinking lights and friendly glow seem to $_2$(**b**   ) from every nook and cranny. A low crime rate and a $_3$(**c**   ) for convenience have made Japan a $_4$(**m**   ) for automated self-service. Masashi Sakurai says Japanese are basically shy, and vending machines are perfect for $_5$(**i**   ). In addition to unusual treats like gluten-$_6$(**f**   ) insects, there are coffee machines that produce latte foam art. But $_7$(**j**   ) food is actually harder to find than healthier options. There's a tyranny of choice, and even higher-end products get the vending machine treatment. Vending machine images are now high art, and are very expensive. Eiji Ohashi has spent 13 years $_8$(**c**   ) images of vending machines all over Japan, but feels he's only begun to scratch the surface.

   5

   10

   15

6. Retelling the News Story

Look at the photos below and fill in each blank with the letter of the appropriate answer. Then use the photos and sentences as a guide to retell the news story to your partner or group.

This news story is about the $_1$___ of vending machines in Japan. They seem to be everywhere. The huge number and $_2$___ of machines make Japan the vending machine $_3$___ of the world.

Japan is a $_4$___ for vending machines because of the low $_5$___ rate, and they are very convenient. You can buy almost anything in a vending machine. Some sell unusual treats like chocolate-covered $_6$___. A planner says vending machines are perfect for those Japanese who are $_7$___ and prefer self-service.

Vending machine images are now high art and are very ₈__ to buy. Japan really is the vending machine capital of the world.

a) expensive	b) shy	c) mecca	d) variety
e) insects	f) popularity	g) crime	h) capital

7. In My Opinion

Write a few words about your opinion of this news story. Then share your opinion with your partner or group.

In my opinion, ...
....
....

8. Conversation in Action

 2-41

Put the Japanese statements into English. Then listen to check your answers.

Jake: Sara, ₁_____. Do you have any snacks?
　　　　（おなかがすいて何か甘い物が食べたいな）

Sara: Yeah, I just bought some. Here, try one.

Jake: Thanks. *Wait. What?* Sara, what are those things?

Sara: Chocolate covered super worms. Don't worry, they're gluten-free, and full of protein.

Jake: *Eww! *Seriously? *I think I'll pass. I can't believe you ate it. That's nasty!

Sara: Really? ₂It's_____! I got it in a vending machine.（あなたが食べている高カロリーの食べ物よりずっと健康にいいわ）

Jake: I'm not surprised. ₃_____. Well, I'm gonna go *grab a coffee and a donut. See you later. （日本は世界の自動販売機の首都みたいだね）

Word Help *Wait. What?:** used before a statement to exclaim surprise when someone suddenly realizes something isn't right, or to indicate confusion about or point out a contradiction in something someone said　*Example: "I'm leaving now." "Wait. What? You said you were going to the party."*

113

*Eww: used to express disgust or distaste   *Example: Eww! I think I swallowed a bug!*

*Seriously?: (Also: "Are you serious?") used to say something is unbelievable or ask if someone is joking   *Example: "I'm thinking of quitting my job." "Seriously? I thought it was your dream job!"*

*I think I'll pass: used to decline, when asked whether one wants or needs something   *Example: "Would you like to try some of my chocolate muffins?" "No thanks, I think I'll pass." / "I'll pass."*

*grab: (informal) to obtain or get (something) quickly   *Example: I'm late, so I'll just grab something to eat on the way.*

Conversation in Action CHALLENGE

Use the vocabulary and phrases you learned in this unit to make a short conversation with your partner. Then practice your conversation with your partner or group.

9. Critical Thinking

Discuss the following questions with your partner or group. Give reasons to support your opinions.

Understanding the News

1. Why does Dana Jacobson say Japan is the vending machine capital of the world?

2. What does the news story say are the reasons why Japan is a mecca for automated self-service?

3. What does the reporter say about the choices Japanese have when buying things from vending machines?

What Do You Think?

1. Why do you think vending machines are so popular in Japan?

2. What are some advantages and disadvantages of vending machines?

3. Have you seen any vending machines that sell something unusual or surprising, and have you bought it? Prepare a short report about an interesting or unusual item sold from a vending machine, and make a presentation to your group or class. Include information such as photos of the machine, and/or a sample of the product, the location and description of the vending machine and product, your opinion of the product, etc.

Dreams Deferred
— College Seniors Struggle with Changing Job Market Amid Pandemic —

UNIVERSITY LIFE / JOB SEARCH

75%
WORK CANCELED, MOVED REMOTE OR DELAYED
SOURCE: COLLEGE REACTION/AXIOS POLL CORONAVIRUS APRIL 10-12

CBS THIS MORNING

CORONAVIRUS FINANCIAL FALLOUT
DREAMS DEFERRED
COLLEGE GRADS FACE UNCERTAIN JOB FUTURE AMID PANDEMIC
CBS THIS MORNING

29% will now conduct internship programs virtually

NACE
Source: NACE Coronavirus Quick Poll, Colleges (results from April 8)

CORONAVIRUS FINANCIAL FALLOUT
DREAMS DEFERRED
COLLEGE GRADS FACE UNCERTAIN JOB FUTURE AMID PANDEMIC
CBS THIS MORNING

1. Before You Watch

Look at the title and photos, and then answer the questions.

1. What does the term, *dreams deferred* mean?

2. What does the information in the photos tell you about the changing job market for college seniors?

2. Word Match

Match each word or phrase with the right definition below.

(   ) **1.** Hospitality and travel businesses were **devastated** by the pandemic, while e-commerce and food and grocery delivery businesses thrived.

(   ) **2.** We're conducting a **poll** to find out what people think about the government's new DX scheme.

(   ) **3.** The **abrupt** change in the city development plan caused a huge impact on local residents.

(   ) **4.** She was disappointed by her failure to **secure** her dream job with a top financial services company.

(   ) **5.** She showed great courage and **resilience** by coming back from a losing position to win the match.

(   ) **6.** Bonus payments are great **incentive**s for encouraging people to work harder.

(   ) **7.** If the situation is left unchanged, the outlook for economic recovery seems quite **bleak**.

(   ) **8.** The doctor **reassure**d him that there was nothing seriously wrong.

> **a.** a study in which people are asked for their opinions about a subject or person
> **b.** to get something, sometimes with difficulty
> **c.** to comfort someone and stop them from worrying
> **d.** something that encourages a person to do something or to work harder
> **e.** very sudden and not expected
> **f.** not hopeful or encouraging; having little or no hope for the future
> **g.** the ability to become strong, healthy, or successful again after something bad happens
> **h.** completely upset and shocked, or destroyed

3. Getting the Gist (First Viewing)   [Time 04:06]

Watch the news and choose the right word for each statement.

1. Millions of college seniors are (distressed / motivated / stimulated) because of a job market that has been devastated by the pandemic.

2. A recent poll found 75 percent of college students with jobs have had their work cancelled, moved remote, or (advanced / disconnected / postponed).

4. Getting into Details (Second Viewing)

Watch or listen to the news again. Fill in the blanks and answer the questions.

[CD 2-43]

Anthony Mason: And trouble too for millions of college seniors entering a job market that's been **devastated** by this pandemic. Many are competing with laid-off workers, and some are ₁(
) derailed by the coronavirus.

A recent **poll** found 75 percent of college students with jobs have had their work cancelled, moved remote, or delayed. In our series on the financial fallout from the virus, Meg Oliver spoke to several college seniors ₂(
) in this difficult time.

laid-off
一時解雇された

derailed
望んでいた道から
外れた

financial fallout
財政上の予期せぬ
悪影響

> **Comprehension Check**
>
> 1. **[T / F]** Millions of graduating seniors at American colleges are having trouble getting jobs because of the pandemic.
> 2. **[T / F]** Many seniors are competing with other workers who have been laid off from their jobs, and are also looking for work.
> 3. **[T / F]** Anthony Mason says the series of *CBS This Morning* programs about the financial results of the pandemic virus have been delayed.

[CD 2-44]

Nia Spencer: Cooking is everything for me. It's my soul. It's everything.

Meg Oliver: College senior Nia Spencer dreams of becoming a personal chef. She was well on her way at culinary school with a paid mentorship upon graduating in June.

Then the coronavirus hit, she moved home and now her mentorship is in limbo.

Oliver: How are you feeling?

Spencer: Um ... right now? Very heartbroken. Uh ... I was depressed

personal chef
個別に雇われて食事
を作る人

culinary school
料理学校

paid mentorship
有給で指導を受けら
れるプログラム

in limbo
宙ぶらりんの状態

when I first came home from school.

25 **Oliver:** Nia is not alone. College seniors around the country are ₃( ) revoked, and job offers **disintegrating**.

revoked
取り消された

disintegrating
崩壊している

Comprehension Check

4. [T / F] Nia Spencer says cooking is the most important thing in her life.
5. [T / F] Spencer's dream is to be a chef at a culinary school.
6. [T / F] Spencer was planning to enter culinary school after moving back home in June.
7. [T / F] The status of Spencer's paid mentorship is unclear and uncertain.
8. [T / F] Spencer says she was depressed when she first came back home from school and feels heartbroken about what happened.
9. [T / F] Oliver says other college students around the country are more fortunate than Spencer.

[🔵2-45]

Oliver: Do you feel like the rug was just dragged out from under
30 you?

Bibiano: Yes, very much. I had to move back to Utah within two days.

Oliver: Rosario Bibiano was in the middle of her ₄( ) at a Smithsonian
35 Museum in New York City, when it came to an **abrupt** end.

How much longer could you have survived without a job, financially?

40 **Bibiano:** Um … maybe like two more weeks, so I was really going to run out of money.

Oliver: But the University of Utah where Rosario is a senior, helped her **secure** a job as a COVID-19 **communication specialist** in a new program it created.

the rug was just dragged out from under you
（じゅうたんを引っぱられたように）足をすくわれた

communication specialist
広報の担当者

45   What does it mean to you to be a 2020 graduate?

Bibiano: My **resilience** being proven uh ... over and over again.

Comprehension Check

> **10. [T / F]** Rosario Bibiano was not surprised that her paid internship was suddenly revoked.
> **11. [T / F]** Bibiano had to return home from New York because she could not afford to live there after her paid internship ended.
> **12. [T / F]** Bibiano's university was not able to help her find employment.
> **13. [T / F]** Bibiano says her ability to adapt to and overcome difficult and challenging situations is constantly being tested.

[🎧 2-46]

Oliver: This is the worst-case scenario for the class of 2020.

Katie Abby: I believe it is, yes.

Oliver: Katie Abby is an assistant dean
50   at the University of Utah.
With jobs and internships
evaporating, the university
started offering financial
incentives for students to ₅(
55   ) graduate school. They also helped create
a paid internship program for students like Rosario.

assistant dean
副学部長

evaporating
消滅する

Oliver: What's your advice to a graduating senior when they're
looking at such a **bleak** job market?

job market
雇用状況

Abby: I want to **reassure** them that they need to continue to ₆(
60   ) and we're going to help them the best
that we can to do so. But it's really important for students
to be open to new ideas.

Oliver: New ideas, like remote internships. In a recent survey from
the National Association of Colleges and Employers, 29
65   percent of employers reported they will now conduct
internship programs virtually.

the National Association of Colleges and Employers
全米大学雇用者協会

virtually
ネット上で

14. **[T / F]** Katie Abbey agrees with the reporter that the current job search situation is the worst possible thing that could happen to college graduates.

15. **[T / F]** As jobs and internships continued to disappear, the University of Utah stopped giving students financial incentives to stay in school.

16. **[T / F]** Abby advises students to keep using traditional job search strategies if they want to succeed in a bleak job market.

17. **[T / F]** A recent survey found that 29 percent of employers will now offer virtual, rather than in-person internships to students.

[🎧 2-47]

Miggs Borromeo: This is a great time to really ₇(

) and improve your abilities.

Oliver: Miggs Borromeo is a senior at the University of Maryland College Park. He had been interviewing for a finance job in California, when the company froze hiring. He currently has a virtual internship he's hoping he can extend.

finance job
金融の仕事

froze hiring
雇用を凍結した

Borromeo: I'm fortunate enough to have that opportunity, because I'm still learning even though I'm … uh … I'm staying at home.

CORONAVIRUS FINANCIAL FALLOUT
DREAMS DEFERRED
COLLEGE GRADS FACE UNCERTAIN JOB FUTURE AMID PANDEMIC

Oliver: But a remote internship is ₈( ) for Nia Spencer. She has been working hard since returning home from school, sharing her culinary creations on Instagram and selling food to her community.

Oliver: Do you think you'll be able to ₉( ) of becoming a chef?

Spencer: Yes, definitely.

Oliver: How nervous are you about your future?

Spencer: I'm not nervous at all. I'm basically just ready to grab on to anything that comes to me.

grab on to ~
つかみ取る

Oliver: She has a ₁₀( ). Now, here at Montclair State University in New Jersey, they're advising graduates

90 to get comfortable, and start practicing virtual interviews. Some tips that will sound familiar, good lighting goes a long way, find a simple

95 backdrop, and Anthony, of course, don't forget to smile.

good lighting goes a long way
オンライン上での面接ではよい照明が大いに役立つ

backdrop
Zoom等の背景画面

Mason: Yeah, I really like Nia's confidence, Meg. You need that right now. But as one grad, as that one graduate tells you, their resilience is being tested over and over again, and they're ... most of them look like they're coming through.

100 Thanks, Meg.

coming through
なんとか耐え抜いている

Comprehension Check

18. **[T / F]** Miggs Borromeo was interviewing for a finance job when the company stopped hiring.

19. **[T / F]** Borromeo does not think he is learning anything from his virtual internship.

20. **[T / F]** Nia is more confident now, and still believes she will achieve her dream of becoming a chef.

21. **[T / F]** Montclair State University is advising its graduates to practice virtual interviews, and is offering them interviewing tips, such as using good lighting, simple backdrops, and smiling.

22. **[T / F]** Anthony Mason says that most of the students in the news story do not look like they will be able to achieve their dream of finding a job.

---

 5. Summary   2-48

Fill in the blanks. The first letter of each word is already provided.

Millions of college seniors are finding it difficult to $_1$(s) work in a job market that has been $_2$(d) by the pandemic. Many are competing with laid-off workers, and some are seeing their plans derailed by the coronavirus. A recent $_3$(p) found 75 percent of college students 5 with jobs have had their work cancelled, moved remote, or delayed. College senior Nia Spencer was studying at a culinary school, and was going to receive a paid mentorship upon graduating in June. But when the coronavirus hit, her mentorship came to an $_4$(a) end, and she moved back home.

College seniors around the country are struggling in a ₅(**b**   )
job market, and finding internship offers revoked and job offers evaporating.
Universities started to help by offering financial ₆(**i**   ) for
students to attend graduate school, and creating paid internship programs.
They are also trying to ₇(**r**   ) students by advising them to be
open to new ideas, like remote internships, and offering students interviewing
tips for virtual interviews. The ₈(**r**   ) of 2020 graduates is being
tested, but most are coming through.

10

15

 6. Retelling the News Story   2-49

Look at the photos below and fill in each blank with the letter of the appropriate answer.
Then use the photos and sentences as a guide to retell the news story to your partner or
group.

 This news story is about college ₁___ entering a job market
that's been ₂___ by the pandemic. Their futures are uncertain
because many of their internships and job offers have been
₃___ or delayed.

 College seniors around the country are ₄___ in this bleak job
market. Some universities started to help by offering jobs, and
₅___ paid and ₆___ internship programs.

 Even in these difficult times, college seniors are not ₇___ up
their dreams. The ₈___ of 2020 graduates has been tested, but
most of them are coming through.

a) creating	b) cancelled	c) remote	d) devastated
e) struggling	f) seniors	g) resilience	h) giving

7. In My Opinion

Write a few words about your opinion of this news story. Then share your opinion with your partner or group.

In my opinion, ...

....

....

8. Conversation in Action

📀 2-50

Put the Japanese statements into English. Then listen to check your answers.

Jake: What? Oh, no!

Sara: What happened?

Jake: I just got an email saying ₁_____!
(ぼくの仕事のオファーが取り消されたんだよ)

Sara: That's terrible! I'm really sorry to hear that, Jake.

Jake: ₂_____. And my internship will be *put on hold*, too. What'll I do now? （その会社によればパンデミックのせいで新規採用を凍結したんだって）

Sara: You should go to the Career Center. They have a lot of paid internship and mentorship programs. You can practice virtual interviews, and learn other job search strategies, too.

Jake: I'll *check it out* right now. ₃_____
_____. *Oh, man!* It's so unfair! （パンデミックによって打撃を受けて以来ずっと求人需要が厳しい状況なんだよな）

Sara: I know. It can really *stress you out*. But *it is what it is*, so, you just gotta *roll with it*, be resilient, and keep trying. *You got this.*

Jake: You're right, Sara. Thanks for your support.

Word Help
*put on hold: to decide not to do, change, or deal with something now, but to leave it until later *Example: Let's **put** the project **on hold** until the economy changes.*

*check it out: to examine or try something *Example: Let's go **check out** the new department store downtown.*

*Oh, man!: used to express anger or displeasure about something that happened *Example: Hey, the school is closed! **Oh, man!** I totally forgot today was a holiday!*

*stress you out: a situation or something that makes you / someone feel very nervous and worried *Example: Interviews always **stress me out**.*

*it is what it is: used to say that a situation cannot be changed and must be accepted
> Example: *I don't agree with the committee's final decision either, but we have no choice.* **It is what it is**.

*roll with it: to adapt to a situation despite unexpected circumstances or challenges
> Example: *The main speaker will be late for the meeting, so we'll just have to* **roll with it** *until she comes.*

*You('ve) got this.: used for telling someone they can do or achieve something
> Example: *"I'm worried about my exam tomorrow." "Don't worry.* **You got this**.*"*

Conversation in Action CHALLENGE

Use the vocabulary and phrases you learned in this unit to make a short conversation with your partner. Then practice your conversation with your partner or group.

9. Critical Thinking

Discuss the following questions with your partner or group. Give reasons to support your opinions.

Understanding the News

1. How has the pandemic affected job offers and internship programs for college seniors?
2. What has the University of Utah started doing to help graduates who are struggling with the changing job market amid the pandemic?
3. What does Katie Abby think college seniors need to do?
4. What tips for virtual interviews are mentioned by the reporter?

What Do You Think?

1. Has the pandemic affected job offers and internship programs for college seniors in Japan or in your country? How?
2. What is your dream job? Why? / How can you best prepare for this job?
3. What three things are most important to you in a job?
4. List four job search strategies you could use to find a job.

UNIT 15

Policing in Japan
– How the Koban and Police Force Keep Citizens Safe and Secure –

JAPAN / PUBLIC SAFETY

 1. Before You Watch

Look at the title and photos, and then answer the questions.

1. What is a *koban*?

2. What are some responsibilities and duties of police officers in Japan?

125

2. Word Match

Match each word or phrase with the right definition below.

(　　) **1.** After three months of training, I **was assigned to** the human resources department at my company.

(　　) **2.** Robots can provide crucial help in rescuing **victim**s of natural disasters.

(　　) **3.** I was **scared** to death when I saw someone approaching me in the dark.

(　　) **4.** Karaoke machines have **evolve**d along with the technology of the times.

(　　) **5.** Vaccinated travelers **are** no longer **required to** submit proof of a negative coronavirus test result when arriving in Japan.

(　　) **6.** Repairing a vintage car can be **time-consuming** and expensive.

(　　) **7.** You often hear people **compare** life **to** a voyage.

(　　) **8.** The police force is an **institution** that serves and protects the people in your community.

---

a. afraid of something, frightened, or worried

b. someone who has been hurt, killed, or has suffered

c. to say that something is similar to something else

d. to make it necessary to do something according to the rules or for a particular purpose

e. to be given a particular job or work

f. an organization that exists to serve a public purpose such as education or support for people who need help

g. something that cannot be done quickly and requires a long period to complete

h. to change or develop slowly into a better, more complex, or more advanced state

---

3. Getting the Gist (First Viewing) [Time 05:46]

Watch the news and choose the right word for each statement.

1. The (basic / core / main) of Japanese law enforcement is the *koban*, or police box.

2. The most popular Japanese police service is (managing / performing / planning) what could be the world's biggest, most efficient Lost and Found.

4. Getting into Details (Second Viewing)

WEB動画 DVD CD 2-52~55

Watch or listen to the news again. Fill in the blanks and answer the questions.

[CD 2-52]

Jane Pauley: Japan is one of the $_1$( ) in the world. And its police seem to keep it that way, while almost never firing a shot. Lucy Craft goes on patrol, with the Tokyo police.

firing a shot	発砲する

5 **Lucy Craft:** The essence of Japanese law enforcement is here at the *koban,* or police box. Besides more than 1,000 police stations, Japan operates 6,000 *koban,* and an equal number of smaller rural posts blanketing $_2$( ) of the

10 country. Close to half of the nation's cops **are assigned to** one.

law enforcement	法の執行機関、警察
Besides ~	～以外に
rural posts	田舎の駐在所・詰所
blanketing ~	～をカバーする

Comprehension Check

1. [T / F] Jane Pauley says Japan is one of the safest countries in the world because the police never use firearms.
2. [T / F] The foundation of law enforcement in Japan is the *koban,* or police box.
3. [T / F] There are more *koban* than police stations in Japan.
4. [T / F] There are *koban* and smaller rural police posts everywhere in Japan.
5. [T / F] Nearly half of Japan's police force is assigned to a *koban.*

[CD 2-53]

Craft: Officer Maika Suzuki says the *koban* puts police **at arm's**
15 **reach** in a crisis.

at arm's reach	腕を伸ばせば届く距離に

Maika Suzuki (voiceover): Dialing $_3$( ) seems easy, but sometimes **victim**s are too **scared** to call from home, or maybe they're not sure if their problem is really an emergency. So they come
20 down to the *koban.*

Craft: *Koban* operate like mini police stations. Their responsibilities are vast,

127

extending far beyond handing out traffic tickets and
traditional law enforcement. Cops have **evolve**d to
become a kind of one-stop-shopping for ₄(

), whether it's giving street
directions, finding a hotel room, lending carfare to
cash-strapped commuters, or even patiently listening to
marital spats.

Craft: But by far, the most popular police service is running what
could be the world's biggest, most efficient Lost and
Found.

Oh my God! This whole floor is just for umbrellas?

Last year, the Tokyo Police Department collected nearly
three million items, including almost ₅(

) umbrellas, from public transit and parks,
each carefully tagged and logged for easy retrieval.
There are five more floors here, stuffed with everything
from baby strollers to dentures ... not to mention cold
cash, as Tokyo resident Jake
Adelstein found. After he
absent-mindedly left an
envelope of cash at the ATM,
a good Samaritan brought it
to police, who returned it to
Adelstein the next day.

Adelstein: Police are very well paid here. So, they ₆(
) to do their job well. That's their task. It's part
of getting along with the community. If someone brings
something to the police, it gets logged in a file and is sent
up to headquarters, and that thing is tracked until it's
returned.

one-stop-shopping	1カ所で必要な全ての買い物ができる場所
carfare	運賃
cash-strapped	懐の寂しい
marital spats	夫婦げんか
by far	断然、群を抜いて
Lost and Found	遺失物取扱所
public transit	公共交通機関
tagged and logged for easy retrieval	後で簡単に検索できるように標識が付けられ、記録される
baby strollers	ベビーカー
dentures 入れ歯	
not to mention ~	~は言うまでもなく
absent-mindedly	ぼんやりして、うっかり
good Samaritan	善意のある人
gets logged in ~	~に記録される
tracked	誰が無くしたかをたどる

Comprehension Check

6. [T / F] It's difficult to find a *koban* nearby in a crisis or emergency.

7. [T / F] The role of police officers in Japan has developed through the *koban* system and therefore officers respond to a variety of public requests and concerns, making it very convenient for citizens in the neighborhood.

8. [T / F] People who don't have enough money for their commute can borrow carfare at a *koban*.

9. [T / F] Cash that is turned in to the police is not kept at the Lost and Found.

10. [T / F] Jake Adelstein found an envelope of cash at an ATM in Tokyo.

11. [T / F] Being well paid motivates Japanese police to do their job well.

[🎧 2-54]

Craft: *Koban* cops go to extraordinary
55   lengths to learn their beats. They're required to regularly visit every ₇(   ) in their districts twice a year. The
60   ostensible purpose of this visit is handing out anti-crime flyers. And here, chatting with the owners of a coffee shop about their security cameras.

Craft: "With Officer Soda, we can say what's on our mind," said the owner. "He's really like a neighbor. Instead of
65   dialing emergency when we need help, we just call him." Visits like this, while extremely **time-consuming** and somewhat intrusive, are a goldmine for cops, yielding tips about suspicious activity, and building community contacts.

70 *Craft:* Police presence here is so low-key and ubiquitous American law enforcement experts have **compared** Japanese cops **to** mailmen. Indeed, the cops seem to be ₈(   ). On guard at local festivals, helping kids across the street. Gently, if somewhat ineffectually, herding
75   mobs at a Halloween street party, and stopping traffic for a Black Lives Matter protest.

Police Departments create their own cuddly mascots.

---

go to extraordinary lengths
わざわざ特別なことまで行う

beats
見回り、パトロール

ostensible
表向きの

flyers
ちらし

somewhat intrusive
やや立ち入った

goldmine 金脈

yielding ~
～を（結果的に）生み出す

low-key and ubiquitous
目立たなくて至る所にある

ineffectually, herding mobs
効率がよいとは言えない方法だが群衆を導く

cuddly
抱きしめたくなるような

They produce cartoon civics lessons for kids. At least one police force in western Japan boasts a squad of dancing officers — all reinforcing the image of the casual, friendly and ever-helpful cop.

civics lessons
公民に関する教え

a squad of ~
～の一団、隊

reinforcing ~
～を強化している

Comprehension Check

12. [T / F] Police assigned to a *koban* strive to learn everything they can about the area where it is located, and must regularly visit businesses and households within their districts.

13. [T / F] Craft says the actual purpose of police visits to businesses and households is to distribute anti-crime flyers.

14. [T / F] American law enforcement experts have compared Japanese cops to mailmen because the police are generally inconspicuous, and seem to be everywhere.

15. [T / F] The police produce anime programs that teach kids about the rights and duties of citizenship.

[🎧 2-55]

Craft: No wonder police are consistently rated one of the most trusted **institution**s in Japan. Every officer carries a .38 caliber revolver, but thanks to strict gun laws, firearms usually stay holstered. Instead of lethal force, officers train intensively in self-defense skills for restraining offenders called "Taiho-jutsu" — the Art of Arrest.

We've heard about something called "The Art of Arrest." What is that?

Suzuki (voiceover): It's a set of techniques for ₉(
). I think of it as a [*sic*] martial arts for police. Our job is to protect not just crime victims, but crime suspects as well.

Craft: On this night, police catch a law breaker in the act ... head off in hot pursuit. After a furious sprint, they get their man: a taxi driver nabbed for making an illegal turn. Later the cops quietly break up a brewing fight. As the evening

.38 caliber revolver
38口径の回転式拳銃
firearms ~ stay holstered
銃器は銃ケースに入れたままになっている
lethal force
致死的武力
restraining offenders
犯罪者たちを抑える

martial arts
武術
in the act
現行犯で
head off in hot pursuit
緊急追跡を行う
furious sprint
すさまじい疾走
nabbed for ~
～で逮捕された
brewing fight
けんかになりそうな状況

wears on, they head out on patrol. An inebriated man mocks them, but the cops remain poker-faced. "Don't drink too much," one said.

105 Not ₁₀( ). Critics say Japan has too many cops, and that officers don't have enough to do. Japanese citizens essentially police themselves, say observers like Jake Adelstein, a former crime reporter.

Adelstein: Japan isn't a religious nation, but it is a superstitious
110 nation. And I really believe that people believe that there's karmic payback for what you do, good and bad. And I think that's a powerful tool in making
115 people behave.

Craft: In 2020, good Samaritans handed in nearly $30 million to Tokyo police. And last year, for the sixth year in a row, Japan had ₁₁( ) since World War II — cementing its reputation as "Heaven for Cops."

wears on
時がゆっくり過ぎる
inebriated man
mocks them
酔っ払いが彼らをか
らかう

observers
観察者

karmic payback
因果応報の結果

handed in ~
～を届け出た
for the sixth year
in a row
連続して6年となる
cementing ~
～を固めた結果と
なった

Comprehension Check

16. [T / F] Because of its casual, friendly, and ever-helpful image, the reporter says it is not surprising that the Japanese Police Force ranks as one of the most trusted organizations in Japan.

17. [T / F] Officers are trained in self-defense techniques such as Taiho-jutsu, which enables them to restrain offenders without having to use deadly force, like firearms.

18. [T / F] Some people complain that more police are needed in Japan because officers have too much to do.

19. [T / F] Some observers of crime in Japan, like Jake Adelstein, say the reason Japanese seem to police themselves is because Japanese believe in karma: the actions you take towards others will have consequences for yourself.

20. [T / F] Japan has had the lowest crime rate in the world since World War II.

 2-56

Fill in the blanks. The first letter of each word is already provided.

Japan is one of the safest countries in the world, though its police almost never fire a shot. The essence of Japanese law enforcement is the *koban,* or police box. There are *koban* and smaller rural police posts everywhere in Japan. Almost half of the nation's cops are 1(a   ) to one. Sometimes 2(v   ) are too scared to call the police from home, or are not sure 5 if their problem is an emergency. So, they come down to the *koban*. Officers assigned to *koban* are 3(r   ) to regularly visit every business and household in their districts twice a year. While time-4(c   ), these visits are a goldmine of information for cops, and help build community contacts. Cops have 5(e   ) to become a kind of one-stop-shopping 10 for problems large and small. The most popular police service is the Lost and Found. Police departments create their own cuddly mascots, and produce cartoon civics lessons for kids. The police are consistently rated one of the most trusted 6(i   ) in Japan. Critics say Japan has too many cops. Japanese cops have been 7(c   ) to mailmen, because they are 15 low-key and seem to be everywhere. Some observers of crime in Japan say the Japanese seem to police themselves because of their belief in karma. Whatever the reason, Japan has had the lowest crime in the world for the last six years in a 8(r   ).

6. Retelling the News Story

 2-57

Look at the photos below and fill in each blank with the letter of the appropriate answer. Then use the photos and sentences as a guide to retell the news story to your partner or group.

This is a news story about policing in Japan. Japan is one of the safest countries in the world. The ₁___ of the Japanese police ₂___ is the *koban*.

Koban officers are required to regularly visit businesses and ₃___ in their districts. These visits help them get information and build ₄___ contacts.

The police have various duties and help people with problems large and small. The most popular police ₅___ is the Lost and Found. Officers almost never use firearms. The police are consistently rated one of the most trusted ₆___ in Japan.

Some crime observers say the reason the crime ₇___ in Japan is so low, is that Japanese people police themselves because they believe in karmic ₈___.

a) institutions	b) payback	c) community	d) force
e) rate	f) service	g) households	h) essence

7. In My Opinion

Write a few words about your opinion of this news story. Then share your opinion with your partner or group.

In my opinion, ...

....

....

8. Conversation in Action **2-58**

Put the Japanese statements into English. Then listen to check your answers.

Sara: *That's weird*. I can't find my wallet.

Jake: What? Are you sure? ₁_____ ?
    （一番最後に見たのはいつなの）

Sara: Umm ... let me think. At the station. I must have dropped it somewhere *on the way* to class. It has everything in it! My bank card, my money, driver's license ... everything! *Oh my God!* What am I gonna do?

Jake: Don't panic, Sara. ₂_____ *turned it in*. （誰か届けてくれているか確認するために交番まで行ってみようよ）

Sara: I'm scared I won't get it back!

Jake: I'm *pretty sure* you will. ₃_____ .
    （他の国と比較すると、日本は世界で最も安全な国の一つだよね）

Sara: I know, I know. *Fingers crossed*. Hurry, Jake!

Jake: OK, OK! There's a *koban* close by. Let's go!

Word Help *That's weird: used to express something unexpected, strange or unusual *Example:* **That's weird**. *The lights went out.*

*on the way: the process of coming, going, or traveling *Example: I was* **on my way** *to Jake's house when I met him in the street.*

*Oh my God!: (OMG: email or text messages) used to express excitement or surprise *Example:* **Oh my God!** *You scared me!*

*turn (it) in: to give something to someone in authority *Example: I* **turned in** *my report to my professor.*

*pretty sure: used to express that you think something is almost — but not 100% certain *Example: I'm* **pretty sure** *I'll go to the party.*

*Fingers crossed: used for saying you hope something goes well and hope for good luck; (a gesture using the hand, with index finger and middle finger crossed) *Example:* **Fingers crossed** *that I'll pass the final exam tomorrow. / I think I did well in the interview and I'm keeping my* **fingers crossed**.

 Conversation in Action CHALLENGE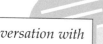

Use the vocabulary and phrases you learned in this unit to make a short conversation with your partner. Then practice your conversation with your partner or group.

134

9. Critical Thinking

Discuss the following questions with your partner or group. Give reasons to support your opinions.

Understanding the News

1. What is the essence of law enforcement in Japan? Why?

2. Why does the reporter say the Lost and Found run by Japan's police could be the world's biggest and most efficient?

3. Why are visits to businesses and households important for *koban* officers?

4. What is the name of the special martial art technique the Japanese police use to keep themselves, crime victims, and suspects safe?

5. What do some critics say about Japan's police force?

What Do You Think?

1. Do you agree with the opinion that the Japanese police themselves? Why? / Why not?

2. Do you think Japan is a safe country? Why? / Why not?

3. Have you, or someone you know ever used the Police Lost and Found service to find or turn in a valuable or important item? If yes, describe what happened. If not, would you use this service if you lost or found a valuable or important item? Why? / Why not?

4. Have you ever used a *koban*? If yes, what did you use it for? If not, in what situation do you think you would go to a *koban*?

Web動画のご案内　StreamLine

本テキストの映像は、オンラインでのストリーミング再生になります。下記URLよりご利用ください。なお**有効期限は、はじめてログインした時点から1年半**です。

https://st.seibido.co.jp

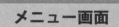

① ログイン画面

🔒 **LOGIN**

テキストに添付されているシールをはがして、
12桁のアクセスコードをご入力ください。

[ ] - [ ] - [ ]

同意してログイン

以下の「利用規約」をご確認頂き、同意する場合は
上記ボタン【同意してログイン】を押してください。

利用規約

1. このウェブサイト（以下「本サイト」といいます）は、
株式会社成美堂（以下「弊社」といいます）が運営しています。
弊社の商品・サービス（以下「本サービス」といいます）利用時の
会員登録の有無を問わず、本サイトの利用にあたっては、
以下のご利用条件をお読み頂き、これらの条件にご同意の上ご利用ください。

2. 本サービスに関して個別に利用規約がある場合、
本規約に加えそれらも適用されます。

3. 本サイトを通じて、弊社の商品を販売する第三者のウェブサイトに
ご案内ないしリンクされることがあります。
リンク先ウェブサイトにおいて提供された個人情報は

> 巻末に添付されているシールをはがして、アクセスコードをご入力ください。

② メニュー画面

AFP World Focus
–Environment, Health, and Technology–

アクセスコード有効期限：2018年4月30日

🎞 **Video**　　🎵 **Audio**

Lesson 1: Global Warming and Climat... >
Lesson 2: Diet and Health for Long ... >
Lesson 3: Self-Driving for the Futu... >
Lesson 4: Sustaining Biodiversity a... >
Lesson 5: 3D Printers for Creating ... >
Lesson 6: IT and Education >
Lesson 7: Protection from Natural D... >
Lesson 8: Practical Uses of Drones ... >

> 「Video」または「Audio」を選択すると、それぞれストリーミング再生ができます。

③ 再生画面

AFP World Focus
–Environment, Health, and Technology–

アクセスコード有効期限：2018年4月30日

Lesson 2:
Diet and Health for Long Lives
食習慣：長生きのためのスーパーフードを探す

推奨動作環境

【PC OS】
Windows 7~ / Mac 10.8~

【Mobile OS】
iOS 7~ / Android 4.x~

【Desktop ブラウザ】
Internet Explorer 9~ / Firefox / Chrome / Safari /
Microsoft Edge

TEXT PRODUCTION STAFF

edited by	編集
Minako Hagiwara	萩原 美奈子
Takashi Kudo	工藤 隆志

cover design by	表紙デザイン
Nobuyoshi Fujino	藤野 伸芳

text design by	本文デザイン
Ruben Frosali	ルーベン・フロサリ

illustration by	イラスト
Yoko Sekine	関根 庸子

CD PRODUCTION STAFF

recorded by	吹き込み者
Rachel Walzer (AmE)	レイチェル・ワルザー（アメリカ英語）
Jack Merluzzi (AmE)	ジャック・マルージ（アメリカ英語）

CBS NewsBreak 6
CBSニュースブレイク 6

2023年1月20日　初版発行
2024年1月20日　第3刷発行

編著者　熊井 信弘　　Stephen Timson

発行者　佐野 英一郎

発行所　株式会社 成 美 堂
　　　　〒101-0052　東京都千代田区神田小川町3-22
　　　　TEL 03-3291-2261　FAX 03-3293-5490
　　　　https://www.seibido.co.jp

印刷・製本　三美印刷㈱

ISBN 978-4-7919-7267-8　　　　Printed in Japan